797,885 Books
are available to read at

www.ForgottenBooks.com

Forgotten Books' App
Available for mobile, tablet & eReader

ISBN 978-1-332-01504-7
PIBN 10268991

This book is a reproduction of an important historical work. Forgotten Books uses state-of-the-art technology to digitally reconstruct the work, preserving the original format whilst repairing imperfections present in the aged copy. In rare cases, an imperfection in the original, such as a blemish or missing page, may be replicated in our edition. We do, however, repair the vast majority of imperfections successfully; any imperfections that remain are intentionally left to preserve the state of such historical works.

Forgotten Books is a registered trademark of FB &c Ltd.
Copyright © 2015 FB &c Ltd.
FB &c Ltd, Dalton House, 60 Windsor Avenue, London, SW19 2RR.
Company number 08720141. Registered in England and Wales.

For support please visit www.forgottenbooks.com

1 MONTH OF FREE READING

at
www.ForgottenBooks.com

By purchasing this book you are eligible for one month membership to ForgottenBooks.com, giving you unlimited access to our entire collection of over 700,000 titles via our web site and mobile apps.

To claim your free month visit:
www.forgottenbooks.com/free268991

* Offer is valid for 45 days from date of purchase. Terms and conditions apply.

Similar Books Are Available from
www.forgottenbooks.com

The Spirit of the Hour in Archaeology
by William E. Gates

Archaeological Excavation
by J. P. Droop

Archæology and False Antiquities
by Robert Munro

A Century of Archæological Discoveries
by Adolf Theodor Friedrich Michaelis

Classical Archaeology in Schools
by Percy Gardner

Anthropology and Archaeology
by Daniel Wilson

Introduction to the Study of North American Archaeology
by Cyrus Thomas

Notes on Iroquois Archeology
by Alanson Skinner

A Text-Book of European Archaeology, Vol. 1
by Robert Alexander Stewart Macalister

An Illustrated Dictionary of Words Used in Art and Archaeology
by John William Mollett

The Archæology of the Cuneiform Inscriptions
by A. H. Sayce

Prehistoric Ireland
A Manual of Irish Pre-Christian Archaeology, by Rev. P. Power

Archaeological Notes on Mandalay
by Taw Sein Ko

Archaeology at French Colonial Cahokia
by Bonnie L. Gums

Man and His Past
by O. G. S. Crawford

Schliemann's Excavations
An Archaeological and Historical Study, by Karl Schuchhardt

Some Observations on the Ethnography and Archaeology of the American Aborigines
by Samuel George Morton

A Group of Nation-Builders
O'Donovan - O'Curry - Petrie, by Patrick M. MacSweeney

Archaeological Studies Among the Ancient Cities of Mexico
by William Henry Holmes

The Archaeology and Site History of 75 State Street
by Michael Roberts

GREENWICH PARK:

ITS HISTORY AND ASSOCIATIONS.

BY

A. D. WEBSTER,

Superintendent of Greenwich Park.

WITH 31 ILLUSTRATIONS FROM DRAWINGS, PHOTOGRAPHS, AND OLD ENGRAVINGS.

GREENWICH:
PRINTED AND PUBLISHED BY HENRY RICHARDSON,
STEAM PRINTING WORKS, 4, CHURCH STREET.
LONDON: SIMPKIN, MARSHALL, HAMILTON, KENT & CO., LTD.

1902.

Soth.
7910
Landscape
25-1923

Printed In Great Britain

PREFACE.

THIS Book is the outcome of a Paper read before the Blackheath Natural History Society in 1901.

The publication has, however, been delayed by the discovery of Roman Remains in the Park, a complete account of which it was considered desirable to include in the work.

I am glad of this opportunity to return thanks to all those who have kindly assisted me with information and illustrations relating to this, the oldest, most historical and interesting of any of the Royal Parks. To Mr. H. Richardson and Mr. J. Cabban, I am especially indebted.

A.D.W.

November, 1902.

LIST OF ILLUSTRATIONS.

	PAGE
Map of Greenwich Park	*Frontispiece*
Map of Park from an old print	5
Queen Elizabeth's Tree	7
One Tree Hill	8
Duke Humphrey's Tower	11
Greenwich Castle, 1637	12
Royal Observatory (early), showing flight of steps	13
Flamsteed's Well	14
Underground Passage in Park	16
Old Water Pipes and Moorish Vases found in Park	19
Holiday Making in Park	20
Easter Monday in Park, 1802	22
Chestnut Beating in Park	27
Montague House, 1786	28
Palace of Placentia, 1434	29
Old Keeper's Cottage	31
„ „	32
John Evelyn	35
Plan of Park about 1695	36
"Seaside" in Park	37
Deer in Park	39
Thorn Apple (Datura Stramonium)	42
Old Spanish Chestnut	54
The Lake in Park	56
Mound on which Roman Remains were found	67
Roman Pavement	70
„ Inscriptions, Carvings, &c.	72
„ Pottery	73
„ Nails, &c.	74
„ Coins	76
Pass to Park, 1733	101

INDEX.

A.

	PAGE
Abbey of St. Peter	1
Airy, Sir George B.	28
Amadis de Gaul	13
Animals, List of	49
Antoninus Pius, Coin of	79
Aquatic Plants	56

B.

	PAGE
Barrows	1, 15, 16
Backhouse, Captain	32
Bastille, Copy of	31
Bath at Ranger's	10
Beauties of England and Wales	102
Birds, List of	50
Blackheath	32
Blockhouses	12
Boleyn, Anne	5
Bolton, Duke of	31
Bones, Teeth, &c., Roman	73
Boreman, Sir William	6
Boswell	34
"Brazen-Faced Walk"	36
Bronze's, Roman	73
Brooke, Sir James	32
Brunswick, Duchess of	28
Buccleuch, Duke of	28
Burial Ground in Park	31
Butterflies, List of	59
Button, Sir William	26

C.

	PAGE
Carausius, Coin of	84
Caroline, Queen	28
Carvings on Marble, &c.	72
Castle, or Tower	11
Challenges in Park	24

	PAGE
Changed Appearance of Park	35
Chapel of Virgin Mary	3
Charcoal, Roman	74
Chestnut Beating	27
Chestnut, Spanish	7
Chronological List of Emperors	99
Claudius Gothicus, Coin of	84
Coffin, Stone, in Park	1
Coins found in Park	19
Coins, List of Roman	76
Commodus, Coin of	80
Commonwealth	4
Connaught, H.R.H. The Duke of	28
Constans, Coin of	91
Constantine the Great, Coin of	86
Constantinople, Emperor of	32
Constantinus II., Coin of	90
Cranmer	35
Crispus, Coin of	89
Cromwell	35
Crypt at Royal Naval College	20

D.

	PAGE
Danes	1, 2, 32
Decentius, Coin of	95
Deer in Park	37
Deer, Purchase of	38
Denmark, Prince George of	31
Dickens, Charles	21
Distinguished Persons in Park	34
Domestic MSS.	101

Drake, Sir F.	35
Duel in Park	26

E.

Early History of Park	1
Edward I., King	3
Edward IV.	11
Eleanor, Queen	16
"Eltham Walk"	36
Emperors, Roman	99
Entomology of Park	58
Epping Forest	26
Evelyn's Diary	5
Exeter, Duke of	3
Exchange of Park	5

F.

Fair, Horn	23
Fair in Park	20, 21, 22
Fasces	67
Fauna and Flora of Park	39
Faustina the Elder, Coin of	80
Fence, Park	3
Ferns in Park	44
Fire House	32
Fish in Park	50
Flamock, Sir Andrew	11
Flamsteed's Well	14
Flint and Stone found at Roman Villa	71
Football in Park	102
Friars' Road	26
Fungi in Park	61

G.

Gallienus, Coin of	81
Games in Park	102
Geology of Park	63
Glass, Roman	71
Gloucester, Duke of	3
Gloucester Arms	29
Godolphin, Lord	5
Gordianus, Coin of	81

Goring, Lord	26
Gratianus, Coin of	97
Grenawic, or Grenevic	1

H.

Hadrian, Coin of	78
Haddo, Lord	9
Helena, Coin of	85
Henrietta Maria, Queen	29
History of Greenwich	102
History of Lee	101
Horn Fair	23
Honorius, Coin of	98
House, Chesterfield	27
" Macartney	28
" Montague	9, 27
" Queen's	9
" Ranger's	9, 27
" White	28
" Sir W. Hooker's	29
Houses, Historic, around Park	27
Humphrey, Duke	3

I.

Interesting Finds in Park	19
Iron, Roman	73
Issues of Exchequer	101
Ivory "	73

J.

Johnson, Dr.	34

K.

Keeper's Cottage	31
Kent Water Works	15
King Alfred	1
" Charles I.	6
" Charles II.	12
" Edgar	1
" Ethelred II.	2

INDEX.

	PAGE
King Henry IV.	3
,, ,, V.	3
,, ,, VI.	33
,, ,, VIII.	5
,, James I.	8, 37
,, William IV.	9
,, of Denmark	11

L.

Lambarde	35
Laying-out Park	5
Leicester, Earl of	12
Le Notre	6
Licinius, Coin of	86
"Lovers' Walk"	36
Lumly, Lady	25

M.

Macartney House	28
Magnetic Pavilion	14
Magnentius, Coin of	94
Marcus Antonius, Coin of	76
Marcus Aurelius ,,	80
Mary of York	11
Maximinus Daza, Coin of	85
Maze Hill Cottages	31
Mirefleur	13
Miscellaneous Notes	101
Montague House	9
Moths in Park	59
MSS. in Record Office	101
Mulberry	8

N.

Nero, Coin of	77
Nerva ,,	78
Newton, Sir Isaac	34
Northampton, Lord	11

O.

O'Connell, Daniel	27
Office of Works, H.M.	101
Old Oak	5, 7, 32

	PAGE
One Tree Hill	8
O'Neil	34
Orchard in Park	31
Oriana	13
Origin of Park	3
Ormond, Earl of	25

P.

Page, Sir Gregory	
Park Gates, Times of Opening and Closing	103
Park Wall	4
Pass to Park	101
Pelham, Lady Catherine	9
Peter the Great	34
Photographing and Sketching	103
Pitt and Wolfe	28
Placentia, Palace of	29
Plague in London	29
Planting Park	5
Plants, List of	51
Plautilla, Coin of	81
Polly Peacham	31
Preface	III.
Princess Sophia Matilda	28
Postumus, Coin of	82
Pottery, Roman	72
Prison, Greenwich	29
Probus, Coin of	84

Q.

Queen Ann of Denmark	29
,, Caroline	28
,, Catherine	24
,, Elizabeth	7, 24, 25
,, Henrietta Maria	29
,, Mary	25
Queen's House	29

R.

Railway Stations near Park	103
Ranger's House	9
Rangers, List of	8

INDEX.

	PAGE
Redoubt at Ranger's	10
Richardson's History of Greenwich	102
Roman Coins, List of	76
„ Pruning Hook	20
„ Remains..	67
„ „ Discovery of	68
Romans in Park	1
Royal Arms at Vicarage	30
„ Observatory	13
„ Sports in Park	23

S.

	PAGE
Sabina, Coin of	79
Sale of Park ..	4
„ Timber	7
"Sand Hill" ..	37
Sarawak, Rajah of	32
Saxons	1, 2
Scotch Firs sent from Scotland	6
Scott, Sir Walter	37
Shells, Roman ..	74
Sigismund, Emperor	32
Silver Street ..	2
Smoking Pipes found in Park ..	19
"Snow Hill"	2, 37
"Snow Well" ..	2, 18, 37
Sophia, Princess.. ..	21
Spearheads found in Park	19
St. Albans, Earl of	9
St. George's Day .	12
St. Mary's Church	29
Stockwell, The ..	18
Stone Implements	19
Straw, Jack ..	32
Suffolk, Countess of	12
Summer House, Ancient	29

T.

	PAGE
Tennis in Park	102
Tetricus the Elder, Coin of	82
Tetricus the Younger, Coin of..	83

	PAGE
Thanet Sand	64
Theodora, Coin of	85
Theodosius „	97
Thornhill, Sir James	35
Times of Opening and Closing Park	103
Titus, Coin of	77
Tower, Greenwich	11
Trajan, Coin of	78
Trees and Shrubs in Park	53
Tree Planting ..	5
Triangle for Flogging	18
Tyler, Watt	32

U.

	PAGE
Underground Passages	16
Urns, Roman, Discovery of	67

V.

	PAGE
Vale of Mirefleur	13
Valens, Coin of ..	97
Valentinianus, Coin of	96
Vanbrugh Castle..	31
Vases found in Park	19
Vespasian, Coin of	77
Vicarage	30
Victorinus, Coin of	82

W.

	PAGE
Water Conduits	16
Water Pipes, Old	20
Watling Street ..	2, 32
Watson, Lady ..	3
Wolfe, General ..	28
Wolseley, Lord ..	28
Wren, Sir Christopher	13, 34
Wyngaerde's Sketches	102

Y.

	PAGE
York, Mary of ..	11

Greenwich Park and its History.

Early History.

Of the early history of what is now known as Greenwich Park, but which was formerly a part of Blackheath, we are, unfortunately, to a great extent, ignorant, though that in days long past the Romans, Saxons, and Danes occupied the land, and here had many a sanguinary conflict with the skin-clad natives we have ample proof. Thus, according to the best authority, the barrows at Crooms Hill link the Park with the early British (several stone implements and flint chippings were found in the Park at Crooms Hill in 1846, and a stone coffin in 1873), the recently discovered Roman Villa with the time of Cæsar, while of the Saxons and Danes there are numerous traces both at Blackheath and Greenwich.

Grenawic, or Grenevic, as the place was called by the Saxons, may be literally translated as the green village, or town—a name that was certainly well bestowed on the beautifully situated verdant fields which skirted that part of the River Thames. As far as can be ascertained, the earliest mention of the name Greenwich is in September, 918, when it was given to the Abbey of St. Peter, at Ghent, by Elstrudis, the daughter of King Alfred, the grant being confirmed by King Edgar in 964.

The Roman occupation of Greenwich Park, judging from the numerous coins and other remains which have been found, must have taken place shortly after their first visit to Britain, and extended over a period of fully four hundred years, while the site of Watling Street, or the Roman road from

London to Dover, still further lends confirmation to the statement. By most writers Watling Street is stated to have passed over Blackheath, nearly in the same course as that followed by the present Old Dover Road. For various reasons I am inclined to doubt the accuracy of this course, my own opinion being that it intersected the Park from Westcombe to nearly where the northern entrance gate to the Park is now situated, crossing the main avenue near the drinking fountain, skirting the barrows, Snowhill and the Snowwell, where remains of it may still be traced, and joining Silver Street (now Nevada Street) at the northern end of the Park. As well as the remains of the road, there are many facts which would warrant us in following this route, such as the Roman remains at Westcombe and within the Park, and the names of Snow Hill and Silver Street, both of which, but the latter in particular, are invariably connected with the Roman occupation of this country, or, as Dr. Pring puts it—"Silver Street is always suggestive of the footprints of the Romans."

We know little of the Saxon occupation of Greenwich further than the name, from which it is to be inferred that these early visitors pitched their wandering camp by the fertile river side, previous to settling down to peaceful occupation of the country.

During the reign of King Ethelred II., the Danish fleet was several times stationed in the Thames at Greenwich, while the army encamped on the hill above, from which centre they made frequent marauding excursions to the country around. They were at Greenwich in 1011, 1012, 1013, and 1014. Both on Blackheath and in Greenwich Park numerous remains of Danish entrenchments are still pointed out; while the names East*combe* and West*combe* are other and unmistakeable evidences of the Danes at Greenwich.

Edward I. is supposed to have had a residence here about 1300, when that King made an offering of 7s. at each of the holy crosses in the Chapel of the Virgin Mary at Greenwich; while Henry IV. dates his will, in 1408, from his manor at Greenwich. Henry V. granted the manor to the Duke of Exeter, after whose death, in 1417, it came into the hands of Humphrey, Duke of Gloucester, uncle to Henry VI., who, in the year 1433, gave the Duke licence to fortify and embattle his manor house, and to make Greenwich Park.

Origin of the Park.

"Please it unto the King our Sovereign Lord that of his special grace, and of the assent of his Lords spiritual and temporal, and of the Commons in this present Parliament, being: To grant to Humphrey, Duke of Gloucester, and Eleanor, his wife, a license to enclose two hundred acres of their land, pasture, wood, heath, virses and gorse thereof, to make a park in Greenwich; and by the same authority to make towers there of stone and lime after the form and tenure of a schedule to this present bill annexed, without fee or fine thereof to you to be paid." — Petitiones in Parliament (15 Henry VI.).

The Park was enclosed with a wooden fence by Humphrey, Duke of Gloucester, in 1433, and walled around by King James, at a cost of £2,001 15s. 11½d. The wall was commenced in 1619 and finished about 1625, — at least on the 29th of January in that year, according to the Issues of the Exchequer, we find an order to pay Lady Watson the above-named sum, which her late husband, Sir Thomas Watson, expended building a brick wall around Greenwich Park. But this was not the only expenditure in connection with the walling, as from the works account it will be found that a number of labourers were employed for levelling the banks inside and outside the wall at a total expenditure of £157 8s. 8d. The total length of the wall is about two miles, and it averages 12ft. in height. During recent years several alterations have been made in the Park wall. In 1699, Sir Gregory Page placed iron gates in the Park wall opposite his house at what is now known as Creed Place, or Maze Hill Station entrance; and in 1823, when the cottage on the angle by these gates was pulled down, the parish agreed to put up an iron railing in the corner. In 1776 a portion of the wall towards Blackheath was taken down and iron railings substituted, in order that a better view of the Park could be obtained from certain houses on the heath. This was at a part about midway between Vanbrugh and Westcombe Park gates, the place being readily indicated by the new portion of wall which was erected when the iron fencing, for some reason, was done away with. Towards the end of 1839, part of the Park wall by the Circus gate, Crooms Hill, was taken down and iron railings substituted, this being done by voluntary subscription; and, in 1841, another part higher up on Crooms Hill was treated in a similar way. In 1855 new iron gates and fencing were erected at Blackheath entrance to the Park, and the old gates of wood—one double for vehicular traffic and another single for pedestrians—done away with. During the Commonwealth (1653) Parliament decided to sell the greater part of the Royal Estate at Greenwich, including the Park, but although one John Parker, of Hackney, did buy the Queen's House, Park, Castle, Lodge, trees and pollards, ninety-six deer, and a small stock of conies, for £5,778 10s. 1d., it does not

GREENWICH PARK.

From an old print in possession of the Astronomer Royal.

appear that the money was ever paid, and the sale being cancelled in 1656, it was declared that the Palace and Park were fit for the Protector and should be reserved for him.

After Cromwell's death it was in deliberation to exchange Greenwich Park, with the City of London, for New Richmond Park.

Laying Out the Park.

When taken from Blackheath the Park wore a very wild and common-like appearance, being covered in parts with scrub oak, thorns, birch, gorse, broom, and heath. There were a number of fine old oaks in the Park about 1519, also remarkable thorns, the majority of which have disappeared. In 1610 thirty-three pounds were paid for trees and plants; and Barclay, writing in 1614, says that, from the high ground, Greenwich looked like a garden, and the roads were lined with avenues of tall poplars. Lord Godolphin, in 1611, states that the beautiful grove under Greenwich Castle had been, sometime before this, demolished in the general destruction made of the Royal Parks, Woods, and Forests. The old tree beneath which Henry VIII. danced with Anne Boleyn, and whose hollow trunk was afterwards used as a prison, is still standing, although quite dead, and there are other oaks and chestnuts of about a similar age. Tree-planting commenced in earnest about 1664, and in "Evelyn's Diary" we find that the noble avenues of chestnut and elm date their origin from that year, for he writes, March 4th, 1664:—"This Spring I planted the home field and west field, about Sayes Court, with elms, being the same year that the elms were planted by His Majesty in Greenwich Park." In the reign of Charles I. the Park was re-formed and laid out by Sir William Boreman—appointed keeper August, 1665—in accordance with the designs of the famous landscape gardener, Le Notre, who laid out the Palace Gardens at Versailles. Boreman planted about 600 elms and completed the avenues of Spanish chestnut, which latter he brought from Lesnes Abbey, as well as planted birch trees, quicksets, ivy berries, privie, and ashen keys. The coppices in the east and west wildernesses (where Ranger's and Deer Park now are) were formed by Boreman between 1661 and 1662. Five hundred great elms for the terrace walks cost 17d. each; other plants came from Kidbrook and Eltham. The expenditure for this planting was £545, and was carried on till about 1665, during which time, in addition to the elms and chestnuts, sixteen coppices and some dwarf orchards were made and a house was built. This house, called a keeper's cottage, was in the N.E. angle at Maze Hill, and was built in 1661. The terraces, which may still be seen on the rising ground between the Queen's House and the Royal Observatory, were also made by Boreman; and at the same time several ground inequalities were levelled, and twelve ascents made from the bottom to the top of the hill, which, with filling part of the great pit, cutting and carrying turf, cost £543 2s. 6d. The terraces were forty yards wide, and planted on either side with a row of Scotch fir trees, which were brought from Scotland by General Monk, in 1664. These trees were planted twenty-four feet apart, and in continuation of the outer lines of those forming the Blackheath Avenue. As late as forty years ago the lines of fir were quite complete, the gravelly soil and airy situation having been conducive to their rapid growth and perfect development, for we find that many of the stems measured four feet in diameter at ground level. With the impurities of the atmosphere,

Photo by Sturdee.

QUEEN ELIZABETH'S TREE.

which have become very pronounced during the past half-century, the Scotch pines gradually gave way, and the last were felled about eight years ago. At the instigation of Sir William Boreman much large timber was cut down in the Park from about 1660 onwards. A number of the elms were sold at £5 each, and an oak at £14; while, from the Wilderness, trees to the value of £100 were removed, and from another part the receipts were £95. This is conclusive proof that large and valuable timber was growing in the Park at that early date. The old oak referred to, beneath which Royalty have frequently congregated, must, in its heyday, have been a tree of giant proportions, the hollowed trunk in which Queen Elizabeth oft partook of refreshments, and where offenders against the Park rules have been confined, being fully twenty feet in girth, while the internal cavity is six feet in diameter. A door was at one time placed on the entrance and a window cut through the shell in the direction of One Tree Hill. The interior is paved, and a rustic seat placed around, on which fifteen persons can sit with comfort. The tree is quite dead (the last living shoots having been noticed about twenty-four years ago), and is mainly supported by a thick coating of ivy; but although every attention has been given to lessen the wind-pressure by reducing the surface of ivy, it is hardly likely that this ancient and honoured monarch of the forest will remain intact for many years. There are several other trees in the Park of nearly equal proportions, one near the entrance to the deer enclosure being 23½ feet in girth at a yard from ground level, and containing upwards of 180 feet of timber. Another Spanish chestnut growing alongside the Blackheath Avenue, near the main entrance, is fully 20 feet in girth, and contains 200 feet of timber. The spirally twisted stems, many with immense protuberances at the base, and curiously netted bark, are peculiarities of these chestnuts which have attracted notice on many occasions. Perhaps the largest elms are growing nearly opposite the Royal Naval College, between the Vicarage and Maze Hill, and towards Vanbrugh Gate of the Park, but, generally speaking, the larger trees are in a very unsatisfactory condition owing to old age, decay, and neglect. One Tree Hill derived its name from having but one large tree on its summit, which was blown down in August, 1848. The first mulberry tree planted in England is said to have been by King James I. at Greenwich. Certainly this King issued a Royal Edict, about 1605, recommending the cultivation of silk worms, and offering packets of mulberry seed to all who would sow them. The Park was disjoined from the Palace when the latter was made into an hospital, about 1694.

Rangers and Keepers of Greenwich Park.

The following is a list of the Rangers and Keepers of the Park, dating from early in the 16th century :—

Mr. George Keene	Keeper	1486
Sir Nicholas Carew	,,	1517
Sir William Compton	,,	1519
Mr. William Carey	,,	1527
Mr. William Norreys	,,	1528
Sir Henry Norris	,,	1531
Sir Thomas Speke	,,	1538
Sir Richard Long	,,	1539
Lord Darnley		1547
Mr. Nicholas Dowsing	,,	1550
Mr. Ant. Andrews	,,	

(Mentioned 1612-1613.)

ONE TREE HILL, GREENWICH PARK.

From an old engraving.　　Photo by Mr. Bouyer.

Lord Northampton	Keeper .	1613
(Purchased Park from "Old Lanman.")		
Viscount Cranbourne	Keeper	1614
Earl of Suffolk	,,	1616
Earl of Worcester		1616
Earl of Holland		1629
Mr. Uriah Babington ..	,,	1634
Sir Henry Mildmay ..	,,	1650
Earl of St. Albans ..	Custodian	1662
Earl of Dorset & Middlesex		1690
Earl of Romney	Keeper	1695
(Had lease of Park.)		
Prince George of Denmark		1707
(Had lease of Park.)		
Lord Aylmer	Ranger	1709
Sir John Jenning	,,	1720
Lady Pelham ..	,,	1730
Princess of Wales (Q. Car.)	,,	1806
Duke of Clarence (K. Will. IV.)	,,	
Princess Sophia	,,	1816
Lord Haddo (afterwards Earl of Aberdeen)	,,	1844
Lord Wolseley	,,	1888

The emolument attached to the position of Ranger was £500 per annum—at least Lady Catherine Pelham received that sum, as also a like amount as sweeper of the Mall in St. James' Park. The original house in which the Rangers lived, till about 1815, was the Queen's House, situated at the bottom of the Park, and latterly in what is now known as the Ranger's Lodge on the borders of Blackheath, the first Ranger who resided there being Princess Sophia, who was appointed in 1816. The Crown's interest in the Queen's House was granted under the authority of the Act 47, George III., cap. 52, to the Hospital Trustees. It was done away with as a Ranger's residence about the year 1806, and in order to compensate the Princess of Wales for the loss of her life interest in the Ranger's Lodge, Montague House, which was then occupied by Her Royal Highness, was converted into a residence fit for a Princess of Wales, including the laying out as ornamental grounds, in connection with the house, of an enclosure in front thereof. She went to live in the present Ranger's House when Montague House was pulled down. Montague House was used as the Ranger's Lodge until it was pulled down in 1815. Then Chesterfield House was so appropriated, and the South-West Wilderness was added to the grounds, on the understanding that it should be restored to the Park on the first vacancy in the office of Ranger. There is a curious bath, now enclosed by low iron railings, occupying a position in the Park directly opposite where Montague House formerly stood, but outside the garden wall, which was evidently in use when the Princess of Wales, afterwards Queen Caroline, was Ranger of the Park, and resided in that house. It was discovered in 1890, when a dilapidated summer-house was removed from the site. A doorway leading from the garden to the bath was bricked up, probably about the time that the house was pulled down in 1815. The sides of the bath and the steps leading to it were formerly covered with small enamelled white tiles, the best of which were utilised when repairing the building before the grounds were thrown open to the public. A lead pipe two inches in diameter conveyed water to the bath, but, curious to say, there is no outlet, so that the water must have been removed by pumping, as a small lead-lined, cup-shaped aperture at cne of the corners would seem to indicate. The summer-house which stood over the bath was built of rustic wood, with a slated roof, and seats around the interior. Nearly opposite to the bath is a fort, or redoubt, which was made by H.R.H. The Duke of Connaught when residing at the Ranger's Lodge in 1863.

From an engraving.

GREENWICH PARK, DUKE HUMPHREY'S TOWER

Greenwich Castle.

The Castle, or Tower, which occupied a site where the Royal Observatory now stands, was built by Duke Humphrey in 1433, and repaired, or partly rebuilt, by Henry VIII. This building would appear to have had four distinct phases of history. Duke Humphrey, in 1433, erected a square buttressed tower with a window facing the river, which Henry VIII., about 1500, rebuilt and added to, the additions and alterations having extended over a period of several years.

About the beginning of the seventeenth century, Lord Northampton still further enlarged and beautified the Castle, where he occasionally resided when Ranger of the Park. Sometimes the Castle was used as a dwelling-place, sometimes as a prison, and at others as a place of defence. Puttenham, in his "Art of English Poesie" (1589), says that Henry VIII., having Sir Andrew Flamock, standard-bearer, on his barge going from Westminster to Greenwich to visit a lady whom the King loved and lodged in this Tower, on coming within sight of it, challenged Flamock to rhyme, and began with—

"Within this towre
There lieth a flowre
That hath my hart."

Flamock resumed—"Within this hower she will," &c., but in so uncleanly terms that the King was displeased and ordered him to desist, for the King, although fond of a fair lady, was a wise and grave man. The same monarch used the Castle for storing wine and other delicacies. The fifth daughter of Edward IV., Mary of York, who was betrothed to the King of Denmark, died in the Castle in 1482, at the age of ten years, where she had been removed on account of the pleasant view and fresh currents of air for which the Tower was justly celebrated. In 1579, the Earl of

Leicester, after his marriage with the Countess of Essex, was confined in the Castle by order of Queen Elizabeth, whose displeasure he incurred by the union. The Countess of Suffolk died in the Castle in 1655. Although the original building of Duke Humphrey consisted of but a single tower with moat around, yet in Henry VIII.'s time it had been converted into rather a commodious and pleasant residence, including a double tower and adjoining buildings, which were embattled, and, for the greater part, four storeys in height. It had a gate lodge, was surrounded by an open wood fence, and planted with trees and shrubs. It was accounted a place of some military strength and considerable importance, for we find that Parliament, wishing to secure the forts and places of strength on each side of the Thames, passed an ordinance (November 15th, 1642) for referring to the Committee for the Militia in London to take proper course for securing Greenwich Castle, with the Blockhouses of Gravesend and Blackheath. On St. George's Day, 1504, the legate's orator, who had charge of St. George's leg when high mass was said over it in the King's Chapel, was greatly feasted in a private chamber of the new Tower of Greenwich, which had just been finished by Henry. A salute was fired from the Tower on the marriage of Henry with Anne of Cleves. In 1649, soldiers were stationed in the Castle to prevent the deer being stolen from the Park. The building was ultimately pulled down in 1675, by Charles II., in order to build the Royal Observatory. There can be little doubt that Duke Humphrey's Tower was not the first building on the hill, else the statement that the Duke was to construct the Tower anew *(de novo)* would hardly have been used; and the prominent situation of Greenwich Hill, overlooking the river and surrounding country, certainly lends favour to the idea.

GREENWICH CASTLE, 1637.

Fro an old engraving.   ORIGINAL PORTION OF ROYAL OBSERVATORY, SHOWING FLIGHT OF STEPS.   *Photo by Mr. Bouyer.*

It has been said, and not without foundation, that the original building was identified with "Mirefleur," a name that had been handed down even to Henry's Castle, for we find that the "Vale of Mirefleur" is mentioned in clause lv. of a challenge by King James in 1606, so that in all probability the valley between the Royal Observatory and One Tree Hill was referred to, and had taken its name from the building on the heights above.

In Hentzner's Itinerary it is stated that "Mirefleur" is supposed to have been the tower mentioned in *Amadis de Gaul*, and to which Oriana withdrew from Court when the Emperor pressed for her hand.

The Castle of 1558, as shown on Wyngaerde's map, is certainly not the Tower of Duke Humphrey.

ROYAL OBSERVATORY.

The foundations were laid in the reign of Charles II., on the 10th August, 1675, and occupy a part of the site of what was known as Greenwich Castle, or Tower. Sir Christopher Wren was the architect, the King granting towards the building the sum of £500, as well as bricks from the ruins of Tilbury Fort; wood, iron, and lead from a demolished gatehouse near the Tower; and promised further assistance. The officers of Greenwich Park were, likewise, to render assistance.

In a letter from Sir George B. Airy to H.M.O. of Works, dated July 1st, 1868, it is stated that additions to the original enclosed grounds and buildings were made—once about 1739, once or more before 1811, and once between 1811 and 1835. Another addition was made in 1837. The handsome building at the southern end was completed 1899-1900, as was also the Magnetic Pavilion towards Vanbrugh side of the Park. The first Astronomer-Royal was Flamsteed, in 1675; followed by Halley, 1720; Bradley, 1742; Bliss, 1762; Maskelyne, 1764; Pond, 1811; and Airy, 1835; on whose resignation, in 1881, the present Astronomer-Royal, W. H. M. Christie, C.B., was appointed.

Much of the original building by Wren still remains, and the twin turrets can be seen as of old. There is a Latin inscription over the original entrance door, carved in stone, dated 1676, which is as follows:—

CAROLUS II^s REX OPTIMUS
ASTRONOMIÆ ET NAUTICÆ ARTIS
PATRONUS MAXIMUS
SPECULAM HANC IN UTRIUSQUE COMMODUM
FECIT
ANNO D^{NI} MDCLXXVI. REGNI SUI XXVIII.
Curante Iona Moore, milite
R. T. S. G.

The late Sir George B. Airy said that the four last letters were understood to mean—"*Rex Tormentaricæ Supervisare Generali*," or "Master-General of the Ordnance." The site of Flamsteed's well, into which the great astronomer used to descend in order that more accurate observations could be recorded, has been covered over, but is marked by a wooden post bearing a suitable inscription. The well was of considerable depth (100 feet), with a spiral staircase of 150 steps, and was encased with brick for about three parts of its depth.

Observations were taken by the Astronomer lying on a mattress and placing his eye to a glass.

FLAMSTEED'S WELL.
From a drawing lent by the Astronomer Royal.

BARROWS.

There are twenty-five barrows or small tumuli on the south-west side of the Park, near the gate at White House, scattered over an area of fully an acre, but many have been destroyed or obliterated by tree-planting. They average from 12 feet to 15 feet in diameter, and several stand 2 feet above Park level. Three others may be seen by the path side nearer to the Royal Observatory and five on the quickly sloping ground to Crooms Hill. One of the old Park roads which intersects this burial-ground may be distinctly traced for about half-a-mile, from near Blackheath entrance, past the Kent Water Company's reservoir to Crooms Hill, where the Stockwell or common pump existed as late as 1706 (Parish Deeds, 1706).

The Kent Water Works reservoir was made in 1846. Excavations for it were first started on the hill where the barrows are, but public attention having been called to the desecration of these ancient remains by bringing the matter before the House of Commons, the site was changed to where it now stands, by permission of the Park Ranger, the Princess Sophia of Gloucester. Twelve barrows were destroyed at this time, a number of stone implements which were then unearthed being at present preserved in the Lecture Hall Museum, Greenwich, while others were taken away by the finders and claimed as private property. According to Hasted, fifty barrows were opened in January, 1784, by permission of the Surveyor of Royal Domains. In some were found braids of human hair and patches of woollen cloth, in another two transparent dark blue-green glass beads, one of white opaque glass, and another of brown-red opaque glass. About 70 years before the date of this search, one Hearn, a park keeper, had opened several of these barrows, and no doubt removed many valuable relics. By several writers these barrows are supposed to be the burial-places of the Danes, who were encamped on Blackheath in 1011; by others, that they contain the remains of the soldiers who were killed at the battle on Blackheath in 1497. Almost the entire skeleton of a man was found in one of the barrows, an illustration of which has been preserved.

Mr. Payne, The Precincts, Rochester (Secretary of Kent Archæological Society), has twice visited these barrows, and is strongly of opinion that they have no connection with the Danes, but are of much earlier date. Until, however, a careful examination by competent persons is undertaken, no definite statement can be made, although recent finds distinctly point to their being of early British origin.

Underground Passages and Conduits.

There are several of these in the Park, one leading from beside the standard reservoir, opposite Crooms Hill, to near the drinking fountain at top of Hyde Vale; another runs from the hollow ground by Queen Elizabeth's oak, towards Vanbrugh Castle; while a third passes beneath One Tree Hill, a branch from which goes in the direction of Maze Hill House. Some of these passages must be of ancient date, for we find that "on 3rd February, 1434, King Henry VI. granted to his dear uncle, the Duke Humphrey of Gloucester, and Eleanor, his wife, permission to construct a subterranean aqueduct between the house he was building and a certain fount in Greenwich, called

Photo by Mr. Strutt.

UNDERGROUND PASSAGE IN GREENWICH PARK.

Stockwell, outside the King's highway, which led between the Duke's garden and the Park, and confirmed the same to the Duke and his heirs for ever." But earlier than this, in 1268, it is mentioned in "Drake's Hundred of Blackheath," that the Abbot's agent sent in his account for the repairs of the conduits supplying the buildings with water, but whether this refers to the Park is not quite clear. That many of the passages in the Park were for the conveying of water we will not dispute, but it is difficult to imagine why so elaborate a construction as that which originates near the standard reservoir, where two persons can walk side by side without stooping, should have been formed for such a purpose. This passage, which is 6 feet high and 4 feet wide, is beautifully built of brick, the floor also being paved; while it is ventilated by three shafts, each 6 feet in diameter, which pass to the ground level above, a distance of between 30 feet and 40 feet. There is an entrance to this passage on the piece of waste ground between Ursuline Convent and Hyde Vale, down a flight of wide brick-built steps and beautifully formed arch-work, with a wooden door, 6 feet high at entrance. That all this elaborately built passage, with its paved floor, perfect system of ventilation, and entrance from Hyde Vale, could have been only for the conveyance of a small stream of water, is highly improbable. This same building passes beneath the road at Hyde Vale, the roadway being supported by massive slabs of granite, many being polished, and onwards to Blackheath Hill, several other smaller passages joining it from different directions. The passage, to which an entry is made in the hollow by Queen Elizabeth's oak, is not so capacious as that just referred to, though the style of building is similar. It is entered by a flight of wide stone steps which lead to a small chamber, from which three passages diverge in opposite directions. The main passage extends in the direction of Vanbrugh gate of the Park, terminating at the bottom of the mound in which the Roman remains have lately been unearthed. About twenty feet from the end of the passage is a doorway, from which point the chamber forms a quick incline to the level of the Park, the floor being paved with bricks. The Stockwell, or common well, as it was termed in early parish deeds, derived its supply of water from the Park, for we find that in 1701 the Trustees of Greenwich Hospital said, in answer to a bill filed against them in Chancery by the Patentees for the supply of the Royal Manors with good water, that two waste pipes always supplied water from the conduits to the poor. The Stockwell stood on the east side of Crooms Hill, nearly opposite Dr. Hartt's house. Sir Christopher Wren, about 1700, repaired the underground passages, or conduits, and added water pipes to two at least. Several of the conduits were abandoned in 1732, and the sale of water to the public then ceased.

In an artificial hollow about midway between the Observatory and Crooms Hill, and hard by the road which intersects the ancient burial-ground, there is an old well, called the Snow Well, about 26 feet deep, the lower half lined with 16th century bricks, and near the surface with those of more recent date. At 4 feet from the bottom a small passage, about 4½ feet high and 30 inches wide, leads in the direction of St. Mary's gate. It was in this hollow that the post, or triangle, on which offenders were flogged, formerly stood, and which was in frequent use up to a late period. Although the hollow referred to is artificial, it is evidently of ancient date, as the oak trees growing on the slope of the hollow—which is much below the Park level—are at least 250 years old. In all

Photo by Mr. Ball.

OLD WATER PIPES AND MOORISH VASES FOUND IN GREENWICH PARK.

probability the well was in use when the old and disused road (which was evidently at early times the principal thoroughfare through the Park) was in general use by the natives of Blackheath and Greenwich.

Interesting Finds in the Park.

In addition to the spear heads, beads, stone implements, &c., which were unearthed when the barrows were tampered with in 1714, 1784, and 1846, a number of coins, some specimens of Roman pottery, and curiously formed water pipes have at several times been discovered, especially when draining and trenching operations were being undertaken. Upwards of sixty coins and tokens were dug up three years ago when forming the shrubbery by the wall-side in front of the Queen's House, none, however, being of particular interest or value. Some date from the Georgian period, while others of silver and gold are of Irish, French, and Chinese origin. One of the tokens was struck in memory of the abolition of slavery; and there are curious halfpenny tokens, as well as brass coin-buttons, and others with square holes in the centre. From a passage which leads beneath Macartney House to the Park, a few pieces of old pottery, including a jug and a vase, an old-fashioned wine glass, and a bridle ornamentation, were taken.

Two vases, supposed to be Moorish, were picked up in the deer paddock some years ago, and a number of Dutch smoking pipes have from time to time been found whilst draining and tree-planting in the Park. One of the pipes is beautifully decorated, and contains the maker's number and mark, but unfortunately it was broken when being removed from the soil. This is said to be the rarest of the Dutch pipes, and is illustrated in "Transactions of the Royal Archæological Society." Some very old water pipes were found in the Park near Crooms Hill, one of which is preserved at the Superintendent's office, and another in the Crypt beneath the Royal Naval College. They each measure 4½ feet in length, with a diameter at base of 9 inches, and at top of 5 inches, the bore being 2½ inches in diameter. Evidently these pipes were cast, the composition being cement, with pieces of stone and tile ground finely. There is a flange at one end and socket at another for connecting two pipes, with a small hole, evidently intended for receiving a plug of wood, in order that the pipes may be kept in position when joined together. Several pieces of early British pottery and a falx, or Roman pruning-hook, have also been recently found in the Park.

But by far the most important discovery made was that of the Roman remains, on the 6th February, 1902, on an artificial mound about midway between the Magnetic Pavilion and Vanbrugh entrance to the Park, of which a separate account is given.

Greenwich Fair.

This Fair, always remarkable for its riotous and disreputable character, came into prominence about the beginning of the eighteenth century, and was held on the 12th, 13th, and 14th of May, and the 11th, 12th, and 13th of October. Even at the Easter and Whitsuntide holidays thousands of persons congregated in the Park, when rough merry-making was invariably engaged in, a band performance being usually given on One Tree Hill. In 1814, the

From an old engraving.　　　NG IN GREENWICH PARK.　　　Photo by Mr. Weare.

Commissioners of the Royal Hospital granted the waste ground between the Park wall and the high road to Woolwich from King Street to their messenger for the purpose of the Fair, the profits arising from the rents of stands to be divided between him and the town constable. There is no proof that the Fair existed before the middle of the eighteenth century; and, in 1772, Lord Dartmouth, as lord of the manor, ordered the Fair on Blackheath to be discontinued, except for cattle, and forbade the erection of booths or stalls. On 7th April, 1763, whilst a gentleman and his spouse were walking in Greenwich Park, the rabble catched hold of the lady's leg, dragged her down the hill and tore almost all the clothes from her back, and during the transaction she lost her shoes and silver buckles. Nearly one hundred years afterwards—in 1831—Princess Sophia, who was Ranger of the Park, ordered the Park to be thrown open for the Fair, but so riotous were the scenes, that in 1838 notices were posted that the magistrates would not allow the Fair to be held, with the result that it was confined to the open space by the street leading from Church Street to the Creek Bridge. The Fair was finally suppressed in 1856. In 1705, an amusing pamphlet, which may be seen in the British Museum, entitled "A Frolic to Horn Fair," was printed; and in 1760 the "Romance of a Day in Greenwich Park" was widely circulated. In his "Sketches by Boz," Charles Dickens gives an amusing account and lifelike picture of Greenwich Fair about 1836; while in 1841, a pamphlet, entitled "The Devil at Greenwich Fair," was published, containing an account of the mirth and revelry which took place at the Fair on Easter Monday. In June, 1774, about noon, a daring robbery was committed in Greenwich Park by four footpads, who entered it singly at N., S., E., and W.

gates, and, traversing the Park in right angles, robbed all the ladies and company who were taking their morning exercises; they passed their confederates and went out each at the opposite gate to which they entered.—(British Museum Newspaper Evidences.) That Greenwich Fair attracted a more than ordinary amount of attention is likewise proved by the numerous clever skits and drawings which, in addition to the above, have frequently been published.

Judging from illustrations, published accounts, and what has been told me by those who have visited the Fair, similar amusements took place to those which may now be seen on Blackheath—in fact, the one is merely a repetition of the other.

Originally a cattle fair, that in the Park gradually developed into a place where general sales, principally of eatables, were held, and amusements of almost every kind were engaged in. Theatrical and wax-work shows were abundant, and even menageries were included; while prize-fighters, thimble-riggers, equestrians, rope-performers, quack doctors, trumpet-blowers, and pickpockets were abundant. The stalls were arranged principally by the roadside from St. Mary's gate of the Park towards the Royal Observatory, on which trinkets, sweetmeats, and gaudy articles of clothing were exposed for sale. On the Observatory and One Tree Hills telescopes were erected, by which for a few pence distant objects of interest could be viewed—particularly the several gibbets, with skeletons attached, which as late as 1840 were still to be seen on the banks of the river. Beneath the old trees, in secluded parts of the Park, fortune-tellers did a good trade.

Tradition says that Queen Elizabeth visited Greenwich Fair on more than one occasion, riding on a pillion, and accompanied by her Master of the Horse, Leicester. The people on these occasions

From an engraving. Photo by J. P. B. Webster.

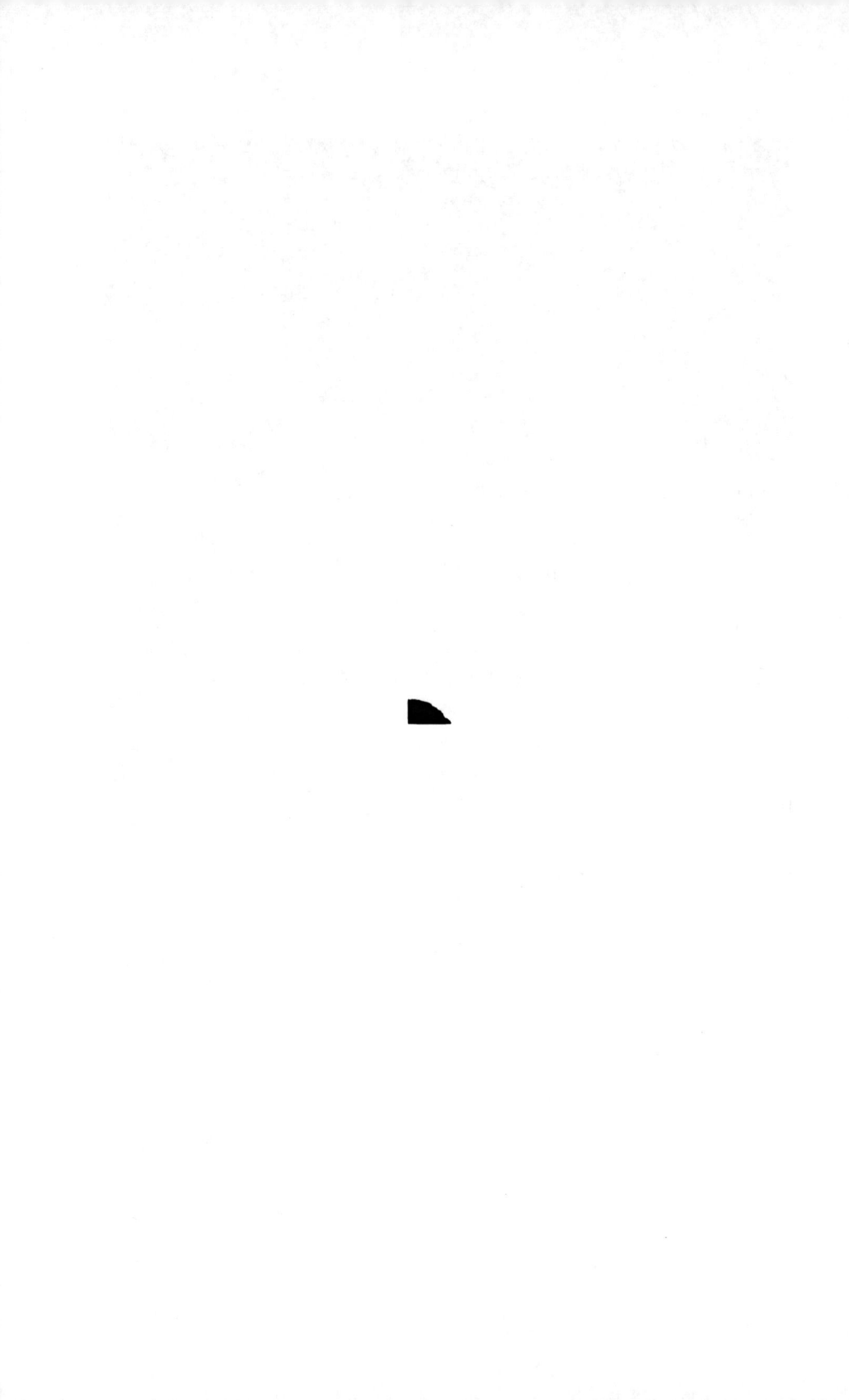

were in raptures of joy, and in their eagerness to get near the Queen, thronged her Majesty almost to suffocation. It is said that on one occasion Leicester was obliged to use his whip in order to keep the people in bounds.

The Horn Fair, which originated near the Park, was so called from the traditional observance handed down from the time of King John, of this merry monarch's love-making to a miller's wife when on one of his numerous hunting expeditions at Greenwich. The miller, it is said, caught the King with his wife, and, pretending to be in great fury, was only appeased by an offer of all the land he could see in one direction, the King at the same time stipulating that the miller once a year—on the 18th of October—should walk to the further bounds of his estate with a pair of buck's horns on his head. To this the miller consented, and being told to look downwards, as the King had no land to dispose of Londonwards, he looked as far as Charlton Hill, and all the land between that and the Point became his.

ROYAL SPORTS AND PASTIMES IN THE PARK.

Greenwich Park was in the heyday of its grandeur and gaiety during the reign of Henry VIII., being bright with bonfires at midsummer eve and boisterous with games at Maytide. Bringing home the May was frequently engaged in by Henry, especially during his first wife's (Catherine) time. Tilting, shooting arrows, wrestling, fighting with spears and swords, and casting the light and heavy bars were all engaged in on the flat ground in the Park opposite the Queen's House, where Henry had a stand put up, from whence the Queen and her ladies might witness the performances.

These games usually took place in February and May, the programme lasting for a week, except Sunday, and from two until five each day. Within two and a half hours as many as 300 spears were broken. A banquet followed the jousts, after which the Queen would present the prizes to the winners. The King was a good shot, and, being powerful and a good horseman, generally came off best in these feats of strength and skill.

"On the 12th June, 1510, the King with two others challenged all comers to fight at the barriers with targates and casting the 8 feet spear, then to fight twelve strokes with two-handed swords. In October of the same year the King prepared a stand within the Park for the Queen and ladies to witness a fight with battle-axes, where the King fought with Guyot, a Fleming." (Hall's Chronicles.)

We find in 1542, in an abstract from the Clerk of Works' records, the following entry:—" Repairing the butts in the King's garden, making two pricks in the Park, raising the ground about the same pricks with sand and turf, for the King and other of his lords and archers to shoot at."

In 1552, there was a great number of horsemen before King Edward VI. in Greenwich Park.

On 2nd July, 1559 (2nd July, 1539, according to *History of Kent*), Queen Elizabeth was entertained to many feats by the citizens of London, and, on July 10th of the same year, the Queen delighted her subjects with much pomp and show, especially military. A goodly banqueting house made with fir poles and decked with birch branches and flowers— roses, gilliflowers, lavender, and all manner of strewing herbs and rushes—was set up in Greenwich Park, as also tents for kitchens and for storing wine and ale.

The challengers were three—the Earl of Ormond, John Parrot, and Mr. North, and the defendants of equal valour. About five o'clock in the afternoon came the Queen with the ambassadors, lords and ladies, and stood over the Park gate to see the exercise. After this the Queen came down into the Park, and mounting her horse rode up to the banqueting house with the three ambassadors, where supper was later provided. "After was a mask, then a great banquet, and then followed a great casting of fire and shooting of guns till 12 at night."

As early as 1520 we find that a considerable area of the ground in front of the Queen's House was levelled for public entertainments and sports connected with Royalty, and that a bridge for ready access to the Park was made about the same time. The bridge spanned the public road and Park gate near where now stands the Queen's House, the road at that time passing through the latter house from east to west. Royalty and the attendants frequently made use of this bridge from which to view the sports that were going on in the Park, and we find that Elizabeth, her ambassadors, lords and ladies so used it in July, 1572, when feats of horsemanship took place in the Park. Queen Elizabeth was very fond of the Park, and Rowland White, writing in 1600, says:—" The Queen dined yesterday at my Lady Lumly's, in Greenwich, and uses to walk much in the Park and great walks out of the Park and about the Park." On the execution of Queen Mary, a bonfire was lit in the Park, and great rejoicings took place, much to the disgust of Elizabeth, although she had signed the death-warrant; and it was from beneath one of the old oaks in the Park that Davidson, the Secretary of State, was sent for to bring the fatal warrant for the Queen to sign, on the 1st February, 1587. Tradition says that Henry VIII., in the seventh year of his reign, on a fine May-day morning, with Queen Catherine, his wife, accompanied by many lords and ladies, rode a-maying from Greenwich to the high ground at Shooters Hill, their way being through the Park. In 1540, Anne of Cleves was met by Henry VIII., on Blackheath, and conveyed through the Park to the Palace, preceded by trumpets and kettle-drums, and followed by all the nobles, "a peal of guns being shot out from the Tower in the Park." They entered by the Blackheath gate of the Park, passed through the Park to the northern gate and through the town, by way of Friar's Road, to Palace (Hall).

Miss Strickland, in her "Lives of the Queens of England," says that "the meeting took place somewhat beyond the cross on the Heath, this cross being on the antique mound, once a Saxon tumulus, which at present may be seen, crowned with a few stunted firs, nearly opposite the Blackheath entrance to the Park." The cross was there as late as the time of Charles II.

It was also in the Park, beneath an old oak tree, that the same monarch set him down to listen for the gun which, by his command, was to be fired when Anne Boleyn was beheaded. Some have recorded this as having taken place in Epping Forest, where the King was said to have been hunting, but the weight of evidence is in favour of the Park.

On the 29th of May, 1648, a portion of the Army, under Lord Goring, connected with the rising in Kent, encamped in Greenwich Park awaiting permission to pass through the City.

"1661—Paid £30 to the Prince's Surgeon for attendance to cure Sir William Button's boy, who was shot in the head with an arrow at Greenwich Tower." (Issues of the Exchequer.)

In December, 1832, a duel was fought in the Park between Lieut. O'Connell, nephew of Daniel

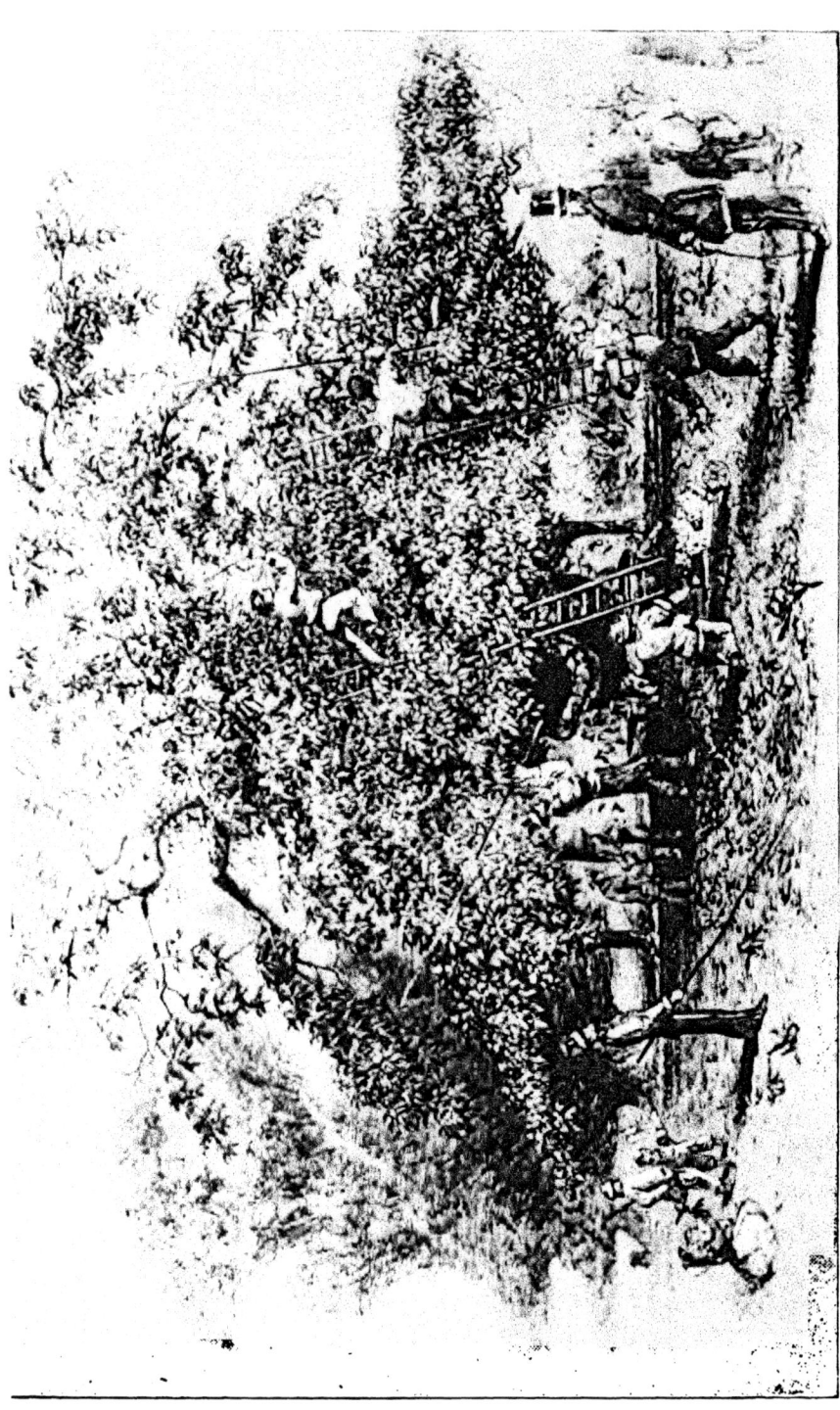

CHESTNUT BEATING, GREENWICH PARK.

From an old engraving. Photo by Mr. Bowyer.

O'Connell, Esq., and a Mr. Carney, when the latter was severely wounded. O'Connell had to find bail for £500.

Chestnut-beating, in order to remove the fruit, was engaged in even at a late date, as we find that in 1846 the Park keeper received £30 towards expenses of thrashing the fruit from the trees.

HISTORIC HOUSES AROUND THE PARK.

The Ranger's House.—In 1688 a narrow strip of land, 30 feet in width and about 1,300 feet in length, on the border of Blackheath, adjoining the Park, was let on lease from the Commissioners of Woods and Forests. In 1697 this strip of land was added to, and its width increased to 80 feet; and it was re-leased at an annual rent of 6s. 8d. In 1753, the strip was divided into three plots, and the centre plot was leased to Lord Chesterfield for 23 years, at the full rent of 6s. 8d. per annum. In 1766, Lord Chesterfield applied for a new lease, and for additional ground, as follows: "A strip of land, 9 feet in width, in front of the mansion, part of Blackheath, and for a space to extend a bow window 11½ feet into the Park, adjoining the back or Park side of house." At this period the ground was surveyed and found to be 557 feet in length by 89 feet in width. A lease was granted for 50 years, at £10 per annum. In 1816, Chesterfield House was leased to Richard Hulse for 17 years, upon payment of a fine of £70, and an annual rent of £18 15s. After the division of the first-mentioned portion of land, three houses were built, one on each plot—Montague House, Chesterfield House, and Macartney House—

the former occupying a portion of the site of the present kitchen garden, to the south-east of Ranger's Lodge. In 1806, an enclosure from the Park of about 15 acres was made when the Princess of Wales, afterwards Queen Caroline, was Ranger and resided at Montague House. This house was assigned to the Montague family in 1714; it had been occupied by the Dukes of Montague and Buccleuch, and the Princess of Wales, Ranger. It was purchased by the Crown in 1815, and demolished in order to enlarge the grounds of the Ranger's Lodge. The house now known as the Ranger's Lodge was purchased by Philip, Earl of Chesterfield, in 1753. It has at various times been occupied by the Duchess of Brunswick, sister of George III.; Princess Sophia Matilda of Gloucester, 1816; Lord Haddo, afterwards Earl of Aberdeen; H.R.H. the Duke of Connaught, the Dowager Countess Mayo, and Lord Wolseley. It was while at the Ranger's Lodge that Lord Chesterfield wrote the famous letters to his son, and immortalised the neighbouring beerhouse in Hyde Vale by the name of "Sots' Hole."

It was from Macartney House that General Wolfe, cousin of Oliver Goldsmith, went to Quebec in 1759, and also from which he set out to dine with Pitt and Lord Temple the day before he embarked. We are told that after dinner, while conversing with the Prime Minister on the forthcoming expedition, he drew his sword, flourished it about, and struck the table when talking of what he would accomplish. The Ministers were alarmed, and, after Wolfe had left, Pitt exclaimed—"Good God, that I should have entrusted the fate of my country to such hands." In 1752 the father occupied Macartney House, and died there in 1759.

Adjoining is White House, the residence of the late Astronomer-Royal, Sir George B. Airy, K.C.B.,

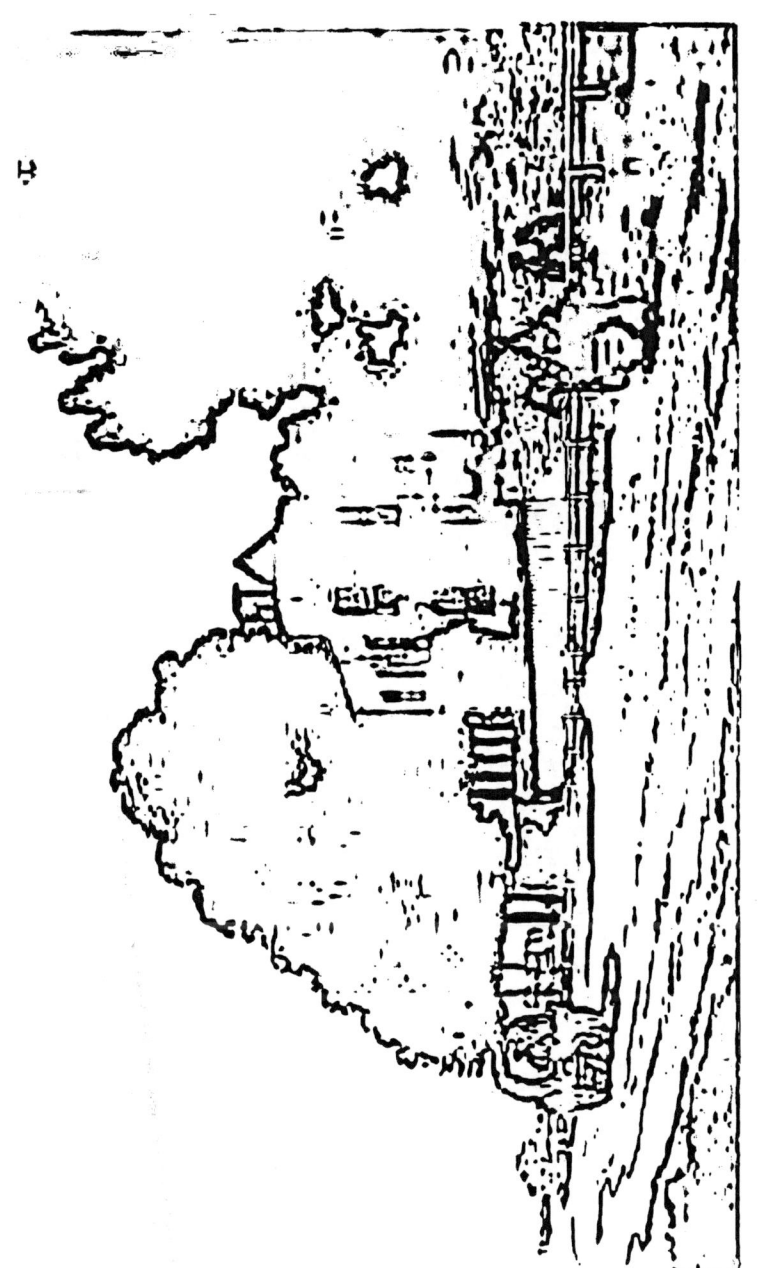

Montague House, 1786.

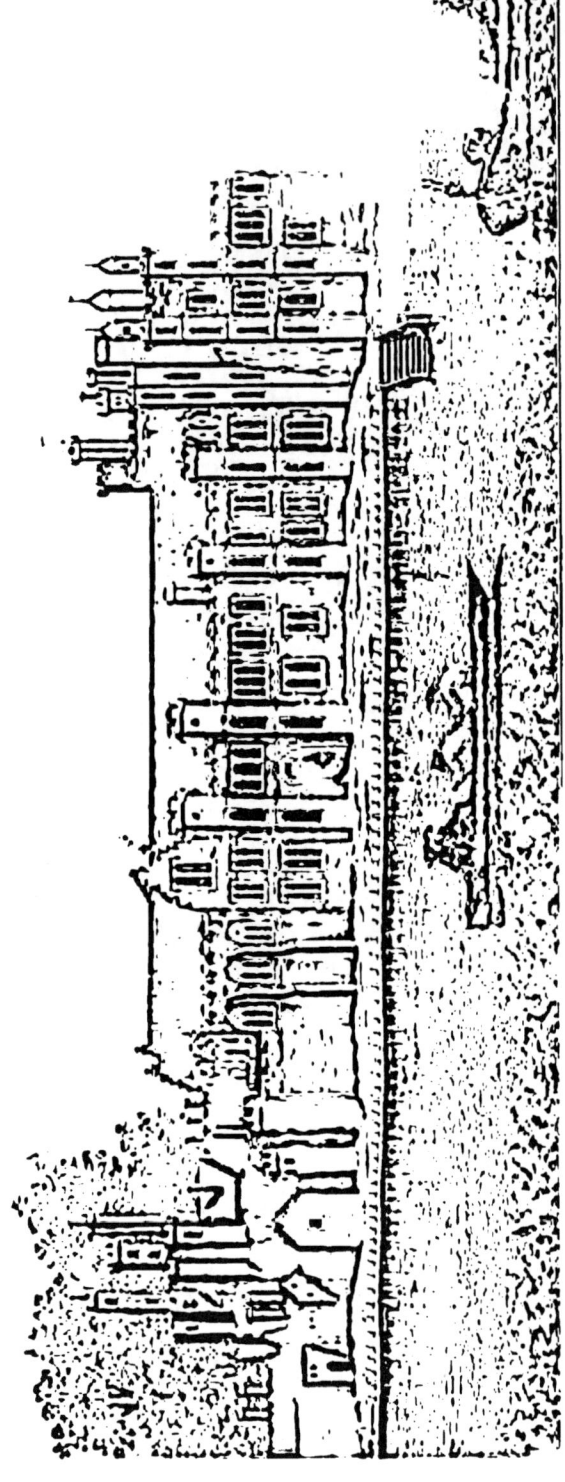

PALACE OF PLACENTIA, 1434.
From an old engraving.

and where the greater part of his library and works are still carefully preserved by his daughters, the Misses Airy. Following the Park boundary, we pass, next to the Roman Catholic Church, one of the oldest houses in Greenwich, and further on the low square building in which the Lord Mayor of London, Sir David Hooker, resided during the Plague, 1665-6. In the garden attached to this house, facing the Park, may be seen an ancient summer-house of beautiful design, dated 1672. Further on is the site of the old Stockwell, or common drinking well of Greenwich, of which I have a record as early as 1434, and which was still in use as late as 1706.

The Gloucester Arms, opposite St. Mary's gate of the Park, is of particular interest, as having contained the old prison where, during the reign of Queen Mary (1555), Protestant prisoners were confined, and lay among the common felons with chains on their arms. I have carefully examined the buildings connected with the Gloucester Arms, and found attached to the cellar a very likely prison, about 18 feet long by 12 feet wide, which, in all probability, is the remains of that referred to, though the bricks do not all appear to be of so early a date.

St. Mary's Church stands on what was formerly a part of the Park. It is in the Grecian style of architecture, and its foundation-stone was laid in 1823 by H.R.H. The Princess Sophia Matilda.

Following on, we come to the old Ranger's House, now known as the Queen's House, the erection of which was commenced by Queen Anne of Denmark in 1618, and finished by Queen Henrietta Maria in 1635.

Nearer the river stood the beautiful building called "Placentia," erected, in 1434, by Duke Humphrey, a part of the crypt of which is still preserved; this having been succeeded by the present

Royal Hospital, which dates from 1705. A gatehouse formerly stood east of "Placentia," which was used for viewing the sports and pageants in the Park. It stood over the Park wall, as will be seen from Wyngaerde's sketch, dated 1558.

Not far distant is the Vicarage, which stands on what was originally a portion of the Park. Regarding it considerable difference of opinion exists, some supposing it to have been the house in which the cook, or chef, to Henry VIII. lived, and others that the Master of the Horse resided here. Perhaps both are correct. On an inner wall of the Vicarage, directly facing East Street, where a portion of the tilt-yard formerly stood, is an interesting relic of the reign of Henry VI. It is the Royal Arms carved in stone. In all likelihood the wall on which the carving is was originally the outer boundary of the building facing the tilt-yard; but with additions and alterations, a second wall was built, which completely hid the arms from view. The late Vicar, the Rev. Brooke Lambert, told me that when he took up residence the carving was partially covered with paint and plaster, but this he had carefully removed, as well as the outer wall lowered, so that the arms might be visible from Park Row and East Street.

This house, formerly occupied by the Ranger's Steward, next by the Auditors of the Royal Naval School, and latterly by a Commissioner of Greenwich Hospital, was sold in 1866 for the Vicarage. It was purchased from the Royal Hospital for £2,600.

Originally the five houses which occupy a site within the Park from near Maze Hill Railway Station upwards were an hospital, the remains of the chapel—which, however, was of much earlier date—being still visible in the grounds of the upper house, tenanted by Mr. G. H. Beaver. The ground on which these

Keeper's Cottage in Greenwich Park.

houses stand was originally (about 1660) an orchard, but at a later date the trees were grubbed up and the whole converted into a burying-ground, with the chapel at one end and a small gate lodge at the other. The present houses are of recent date, and would appear to be subdivisions of the hospital which was erected in 1782. In 1707, Prince George of Denmark gave 660 feet by 52 feet of ground lying by the side of the Park, adjoining Maze Hill, for a burying-ground. Burials ceased in 1749. When trenching and preparing the ground for the adjoining shrubbery many human remains were unearthed, as also building materials from the old gate lodge. The circular pillar by the corner of the chapel is one of the finest pieces of brickwork within the Park.

Vanbrugh Castle, a copy of the Bastille, comes next. It was built by Sir John Vanbrugh, about 1717, as was also Mince Pie House, close by. Not far distant was Westcombe Park House, at one time the residence of William Lambarde, the learned antiquarian, and author of "A Perambulation of Kent"; afterwards it came into the possession of Charles, third Duke of Bolton, who resided here upwards of twenty years with Miss Lavinia Fenton —Polly Peacham of the famous "Beggars' Opera" —whom he married in 1751. She remained here as Duchess-Dowager of Bolton from 1754 till her death in 1760.

The old Keeper's Cottage, or Lodge, which stood close to Queen Elizabeth's Oak, near the centre of the Park, and which was pulled down in 1853, was in all probability that referred to in the sale of the Park during the Commonwealth, and is shown on maps of that date. From a map of the Park, dated 1695, a building similar in every respect to that which was demolished in 1853, surrounded by an orchard, can be traced. Both the old oak and the pump were within the oaken garden fence, the hollow trunk of the former having for many years been used as a prison for those who trespassed against the rules of the Park. Fifty years ago it was also in use as a room in which to partake of tea and fruit, and as an office for payment of the Park workmen. Two persons have told me that they were confined here by the Park-keeper for breaking the branches of the chestnut trees when stealing the fruit, and it is recorded that a sweep from Blackheath escaped from the prison by scaling the interior of the hollow trunk. Sir James Brooke, the Rajah of Sarawak, occasionally lodged in the old cottage; and the widow of Captain Backhouse, brother to Captain Back who went out in search of Captain Ross, in 1833, also resided here for several years.

Close to the Park fence by Blackheath stood the fire-house, a commodious building owned by a Mr. George Shott, where appliances for the old matchlock gun were manufactured.

The adjoining Blackheath Common, from which the Park was taken in 1433, was the scene of many important events. The famous Watling Street, which passes from here through the Park, and other remains, link it firmly with the time of the Romans; while the Danes encamped here in 1011. In 1381, Watt Tyler and Jack Straw had 100,000 men on the Heath; while in 1400, the Emperor of Constantinople was met on Blackheath by King Henry IV. with great parade and magnificence. Here also, in 1415, King Henry V. was met, on his return from the Battle of Agincourt, by the Lord Mayor and Aldermen of London and 400 citizens; and in the following year, the Emperor Sigismund came here to treat for peace between the Crowns of England and France. Henry VI., on his return from France in 1431, was received on Blackheath

From an engraving. *Photo by Sturdee.*

KEEPER'S COTTAGE I GREENWICH PARK, PULLED DOWN 1853.

with great pomp by the Lord Mayor and Aldermen of London; and in May of 1428, Humphrey, Duke of Gloucester, with 500 men wearing his livery, and the Mayor and Aldermen of London, met Margaret of Anjou on Blackheath, and conducted her to his palace. The followers of Jack Cade, in 1449-50, were twice encamped on the plain of Blackheath, and on the 23rd February, 1451, many of his men came in their shirts to the King at the same place and begged for pardon on their knees. King Henry VI. pitched his tent on Blackheath in 1452, when withstanding the forces of his cousin, the Duke of York, afterwards King Edward IV.; and Richard, Duke of York, in the same year, came out of Wales to Blackheath, the King meeting him with 15,000 men. In 1471, Falconbridge encamped here to assist Edward IV., this same King being met here on his return from France in 1474, by the Lord Mayor and Aldermen of London; while, in 1497, the Cornish rebels, numbering 6,000, were defeated by Henry VII. on the Heath. In 1512, the King knighted, on the Heath, a Flemish gentleman, called Guyot of Guy, who was accompanied by 500 Almaines. The Pope's Legate, Cardinal Campejus, was met on Blackheath by the Duke of Norfolk in 1518; while, in 1540, the Princess Anne of Cleves was met here with much pomp by Henry VIII. The Army was drawn up on Blackheath to receive Charles II. on his way to London after the Restoration. To the number of 5,000, the City Militia mustered before Queen Elizabeth at Greenwich, from their encampment on the Heath; and in 1645, Colonel Blunt drew out two regiments of foot and exercised them on this Heath, representing a mock fight between the Cavaliers and Roundheads. About 1800, an inspection of the local Militia and Volunteers was held in the presence of Frederick, Duke of York.

D

Besides the above, many remarkable meetings took place on the Heath, outside Greenwich Park, it being the place where distinguished persons were usually received in order to be conducted with proper state and ceremony to London.

Distinguished Persons who have Visited the Park.

From about 1408, when Henry IV. owned the Manor of Greenwich, and had a royal residence there, until the reign of George II., in the middle of the eighteenth century (1742), Greenwich Park was visited frequently by most of our kings and queens, as well as by all the more notable persons of their time. The consort of Charles I. was the last Royal occupant the Queen's House received, although, as late as 1823, Princess Sophia, who lived at the Ranger's House, passed through the Park when on her way to lay the foundation-stone of St. Mary's Church. The procession, accompanied by Princess Sophia and the Bishop of Oxford, started from Blackheath gate of the Park, and proceeded by way of the main avenue to St. Mary's gate. Peter the Great visited the Park four times during 1698, Sir Isaac Newton in 1694, and again with Sir Christopher Wren in 1700. Dr. Johnson lodged in Greenwich and composed the greater part of his "Irene" in the Park, which he again visited in 1763 in company with Boswell. In 1542, the great O'Neil came from Ireland to offer submission to the King at Greenwich, when he was created Earl of Tyrone, the King paying all his expenses in connection with the visit.

Greenwich was always more or less connected with the Navy, and here, in addition to many of the

JOHN EVELYN.

greatest naval men of the day, Queen Elizabeth welcomed Drake on his return from the famous voyage of discovery. From a letter of Nelson's, on board H.M.S. "Agamemnon," dated 1795, it is to be inferred that he had visited the Park; and we are all aware that his dead body was brought to Greenwich, and lay in the Painted Hall hard by the Park before being removed to St. Paul's for burial. Lambarde, the historian, who was a magistrate of Greenwich about 1570, knew the Park well; and Evelyn, who wrote his famous "Sylva" in 1664, was a frequent visitor, and gave advice to the King in reference to tree-planting in the Park. Wolsey and Cranmer were often at Greenwich, while Cromwell preferred the Palace and Park to any other of his residences. From 1708 to 1727, Sir James Thornhill (Hogarth's father-in-law) made frequent excursions to the Park, as did also Charles Dickens in his earlier life. Sir James Brook, the Rajah of Sarawak, lived in the Park on several occasions.

Changed Appearance of the Park.

The physical features of the Park have become greatly changed, particularly during the last hundred years. Formerly, on entering the Park by Blackheath gate, one was confronted by "The Rounds," a semi-circle of fine old chestnuts, four deep, which were planted when the main avenue was laid out. The chestnuts are still to be seen, some of immense girth, but the semi-circular open space has partially disappeared, by continuing the trees which form the avenue right up to the main gate. At the opposite end of this avenue another great change has been brought about by the removal of the trees facing north, and by the death of the Scotch firs which formed part of the square nearer to the Observatory. The additions to the Royal Observatory, erection of magnetic pavilion, entrance gates, and the making of reservoir for Kent Water Company, and demolishing of conduit towers and old keeper's cottage have all much altered the appearance of the Park during the past fifty years.

On comparing the Park of to-day with maps of much earlier date, the changes are indeed great. The house, now the Vicarage, the site of Park cottages and Naval officers' drilling ground, were all within the Park, while various orchards of fruit trees existed at that date. The main avenue to Blackheath was then named "Eltham Walk," that from St. Mary's gate to the Observatory, "Brazen-Faced Walk," or "Snow Hill," while the road at bottom of One-Tree-Hill was known as the "Lovers' Walk."

What is known as the "old oak" was then, with the pump and demolished cottage, almost hidden by a thickly planted orchard; while the Wilderness, or present deer enclosure, extended to Vanbrugh Castle entrance, there being no gate between that and Blackheath, as there is now at Westcombe Park. The site of the present shrubberies and cottages between lower Maze Hill gate and Maze Hill House was then an orchard, although a little later the orchard was grubbed up, the present cottages, in form of an hospital, being erected, with a small chapel for reading the burial service, and a cemetery was attached. The chapel is still to be seen.

At one time, and not so long ago, the Observatory and One Tree Hill were loose gravel with great ruts and trenches, while the public had no entry to the ground attached to the Ranger's House. One Tree Hill was called "Sand Hill," and that on the west of

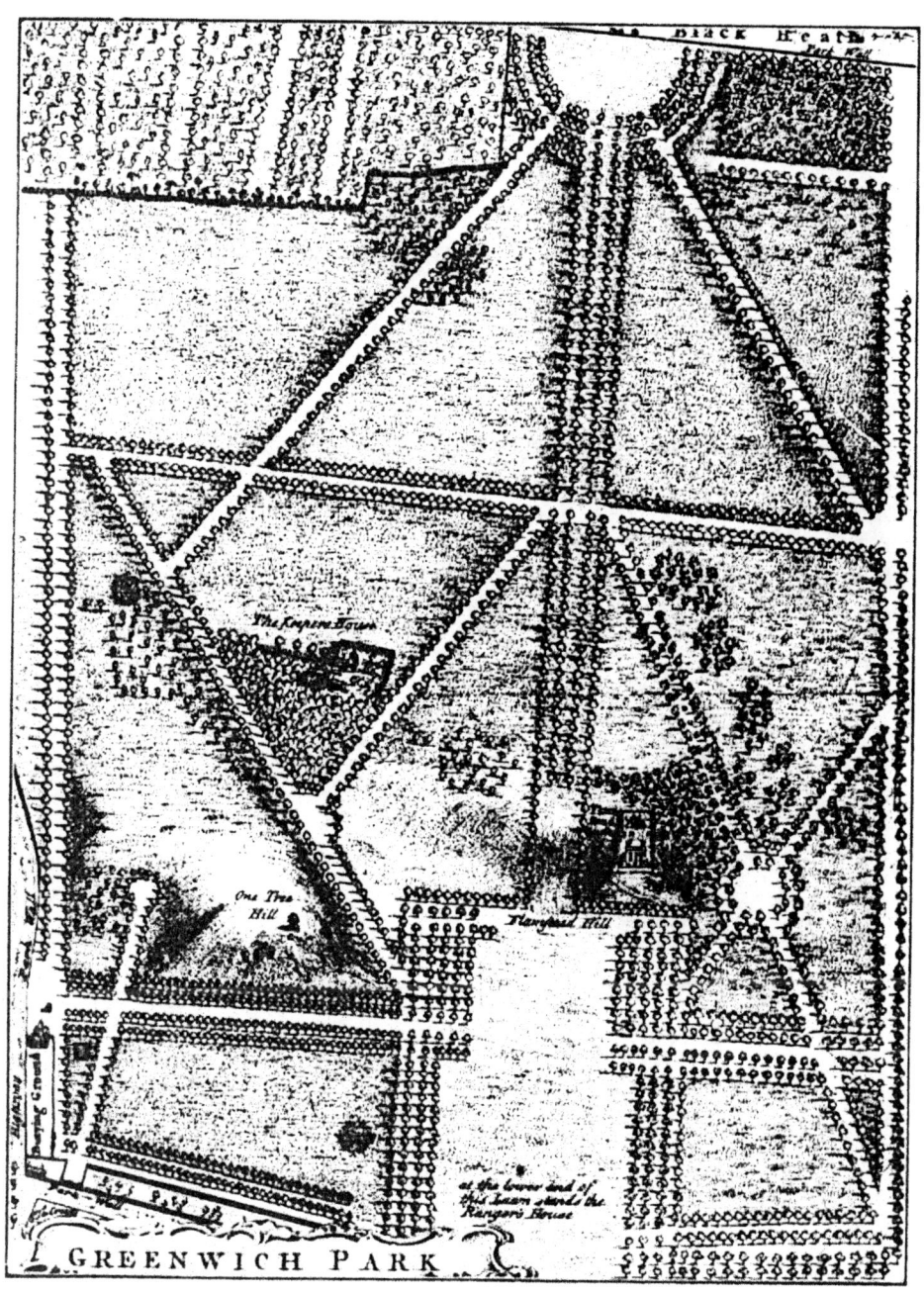

PLAN OF GREENWICH PARK ABOUT 1695.

'Seaside' in Greenwich Park.

Photo by Sturdee.

the Observatory "Snow Hill," from the Snow Well there. From 1730 until 1850 the Park was much neglected. In 1854, the keeper's lodge, mentioned above, was taken down and the site thrown into the Park. The avenues were levelled and gravelled, and the steps on the Observatory Hill repaired; while the ice-house, on the same hill, has been filled in.

The pond enclosure with its choice collection of flowering trees and shrubs has greatly improved the appearance of that part of the Park; while "Seaside in Greenwich Park," where children may play on the clean sand, without fear of molestation, has converted a dirty and untidy corner into a valuable and much appreciated play-place.

Deer in the Park.

The first account we have of deer in the Park is in January, 1510, when £13 6s. 8d. was paid to Eustace Browne for deer to enstock Greenwich Park. In 1518 twenty quick deer were transferred here from Eltham, by Francis Bryan; who, in 1520, received £20 for bringing sixty live deer from Rayleigh Park, Essex. In 1598, the German traveller, Paul Hentzner, when at Greenwich, speaks of the beautiful Queen's Park stocked with deer. The Earl of Northampton took special delight in the deer, and in keeping the Park generally clean and neat, as would appear from his letter to the King's secretary in 1614. Sir Walter Scott, in the "Waverley Novels" ("Fortunes of Nigel"), talks of King James hunting the deer in Greenwich Park.

During the Commonwealth, when robberies were frequent at Blackheath and Greenwich, a troop was

Deer in Greenwich Park.

Photo by Mr. Weare.

are unacquainted with their habits both unnecessary and out of place. That the reverse is the case will, however, be admitted when it is known that of late years several bucks and does have been killed by the too pressing attention of visitors in providing them with food. One died from partaking too freely of gooseberry tart, another from eating orange peel—two hatfuls being found in its stomach—while others have been killed by devouring strips of cloth, paper, and mutton bones. Fallow deer are thorough scavengers, and will pick up almost anything they come across—sweets, bread, flesh meat, paper, diseased fruit, pastry, cloth, leather—and have even been known to act the cannibal by eating venison cutlets. Immediately the Park is closed to the public, numbers of deer flock around the kiosk, and generally scour the Park to pick up anything eatable that may have been dropped, or left by visitors, and that, too, in spring and summer, when fresh grass is most abundant. The quietly undulating, well-wooded ground of the Park is peculiarly suited for a herd of deer, and in order to keep these in a healthy condition the general public should co-operate with the Park keepers in preventing violation of the notice—"Please do not feed the deer."

The Fauna and Flora of Greenwich Park.

To the casual observer the number of wild birds and plants that are to be found in the Royal Park of Greenwich will be considered small, indeed, and hardly of sufficient interest to warrant the compilation of a special paper on the subject. That this is by no means the case will, however, be amply borne out by the following brief notes regarding such ordered to the Park, July 4th, 1649, to preserve the deer and oppose those who came to take them by force.

In 1653, when Parliament decided to sell the greater part of the Royal Estate at Greenwich, one John Parker, a speculator, bought the Park of 187 acres, the castle, lodge, trees, ninety-six deer, and a small stock of conies. Evidently the deer were highly prized, for in a valuation of the Park timber about 1660, it is mentioned that "the woods are for browse and covert for the deer, and ornament and shade for the walks." After this date it does not appear that a herd of deer was absent from the Park, though at some times, owing to want of attention and too close relationship, the numbers were very low. In 1851, some of the deer were transferred to Bushy Park.

Four hundred years have totally changed the aspect of affairs, for with an increased number of visitors and the deleterious effects of an impure atmosphere, the grass in the Park is not what it used to be, and the difficulties to contend with in the rearing and management of deer have greatly increased. Six years ago the herd numbered 47, while at present there are nearly 150; some of these have been introduced and others reared in the Park, the quiet of the deer enclosure with its old oaks and dense undergrowth of bracken providing an excellent secluded retreat for fawning, as also for feeding purposes during the winter months, and an enclosure at holiday times. On an average, from fifteen to twenty fawns are reared each season, and they require to be fully four months old before being admitted to the open Park. The general public have little idea of the care and attention required in order to keep the herd in a healthy and thriving condition, and the notice not to feed the deer may seem to those who

interesting is the fullers teasel *(Dipsacus sylvestris)*, which is by no means rare amongst the shrubs on One Tree Hill. It is a handsome plant, often attaining to five feet in height, and much in use for decorative purposes.

Although hardly recognised as a native plant, the datura, or thorn apple *(Datura stramonium)*, has become quite naturalised in the deer park, the sloping banks of a disused gravel-pit having been known to foster the plant for a full half-century. The large, deeply-divided leaves are very handsome; while the fruit resembles a horse-chestnut, but is far more prickly. The whole plant is narcotic and stimulant, and should not be placed within the reach of children. Curiously enough, the pure white convolvulus-like flowers are seen to best advantage about eight o'clock in the evening. Whether the Lent lily *(Narcissus pseudo narcissus)* is really wild, it would be hard to say; but, judging from the number of isolated clumps which occur amongst the bracken in the deer park, and where it is very unlikely to have been planted, I should say it has just claims to be regarded as a native of the district.

Both species of solanum—the family to which our cultivated potato and tomato belong—are to be found in the Park.

The bitter-sweet, or nightshade *(S. dulcamara)*, is to be seen near Chesterfield entrance, and the black solanum *(S. nigrum)* plentifully in many of the shrubberies and borders.

The meadow saffron, or colchicum *(C. autumnalis)*, is also seen in several parts of the Ranger's grounds— in the woodlands, where it is hardly likely to have been planted for effect. Possibly the common primrose may be considered as natural to the Park, in which it is to be found sparingly; while the cowslip occurs in three distinct places where it is

THE THORN APPLE (DATURA) IN DEER ENCLOSURE, GREENWICH PARK.

Photo by Mr. Potter.

most unlikely to have been introduced by the hands of man. In summer, hundreds of visitors almost tread on the latter plant, and yet for three years it has escaped notice—or rather extermination.

Three species of campanula are fairly common in the Park: the hairbell (*C. rotundifolia*), the nettle-leaved (*C. trachelium*), and the creeping form (*C. rapunculoides*). The nettle-leaved is abundant in several parts of the Park; while within the grounds of the Magnetic Pavilion the deep-blue flowers of the hairbell are a conspicuous feature during the autumn months. Of aquatic and semi-aquatic plants there is a large and varied assortment in and around the pond, many of which have made their appearance of late years since water-fowls have been encouraged, and the public kept from encroaching too near to the margin. The pretty little water ranunculus (*R. aquatilis*) certainly was not known on the pond four years ago, whereas at the present time it is fairly abundant; and this may also be said of the frogbit (*Hydrocharis Morsusrana*), which made its first appearance last summer, although in limited numbers. The yellow flowered water lily has lately appeared, with the less common *Potamogeton crispus*.

The branched burr-reed (*Sparganium ramosum*), the water arrowhead (*Sagittaria sagittifolia*), and water plantain (*Alisma plantago*) are all abundant; whilst the deliciously fragrant sweet acorus (*A. calamus*) is to be found in plenty.

Grasses of various kinds are found commonly by the pond margin; and also the moneywort(*Lysimachia*) with its showy yellow flowers and neat procumbent habit of growth; the marsh marigold (*Caltha palustris*), and the common iris. The only native plants that I have introduced to the water are the greater and lesser reedmace and catstail (*Typha*), the bog-bean, variegated-leaved iris, lymegrass, and the white water lily. All the others have made their appearance—how, I know not; but in all probability as before-mentioned—through the agency of birds. One water-plant I must not forget to mention—the American weed (*Elodea Canadensis*), which made its appearance in the pond five years ago, and so rapidly has it increased that over one hundred cart-loads have been removed during the last and present summer. This plant is of particular interest, in that, although introduced to this country only about forty-five years ago, it has so overrun the canals and streams in almost every part of the British Isles that thousands of pounds sterling have been spent in keeping the waters open for navigation. Its introduction is said to be due to the late Professor Babington, and after whom it was nick named *Babingtonia damnabilis*. It is certainly a veritable pest, as the least portion of the plant seems to be able to root afresh and increase with amazing rapidity.

Ferns are sparsely represented, but I might mention that the wall rue (*Asplenium ruta muraria*), the hart's tongue (*Scolopendrium vulgare*), the Male and Lady ferns, the shield (*Polystichum*), and the common polypody have been found; while the bracken covers several acres of the deer park. One of the prettiest of our native plants is the Lady's bedstraw (*Galium verum*), of which numerous tufts may be seen by the fort in the Ranger's grounds, and of which I am trying to extend the growth by seed-sowing in suitable parts of the Park.

The millfoil, or yarrow (*Achillæ millæfolium*), is found in the same place as the above.

Native trees and shrubs would include two species of pyrus—the beam-tree (*P. aria*) and the far more uncommon wild service tree (*P. torminalis*), of which latter several seedlings have been picked up in the Park. Both the butcher's broom (*Ruscus aculeatus)* and the spindle tree *(Euonymus)* are undoubtedly wild, and the same will apply to the elder and hawthorn, the holly and maple, the mountain ash, broom, and gorse. Seedlings of the oak, ash, birch, sycamore, elm, and beech may also be picked up. Within the enclosure on the Observatory Hill a large number of wild plants are to be found, such as the giant fennel (two forms), mallow, wild geranium, *Achillea* (two species), viscid lychnis, and the bladder campion *(Silene inflata)*. Many visitors to the Park during the past summer were charmed with the pretty pinky flowers of another member of the silene family, which is of Continental origin. I refer to *S. armeria*, which first made its appearance three years ago in one of the borders, where seedlings were produced so freely that last summer the ground was carpeted with the plant, displaying for fully three months a glowing mass of colour. Very plentiful has the American oxalis *(O. floribunda)* become; indeed, in the dell by the Ranger's, square yards of the pretty shamrock-like foliage and bright pinky flowers may be seen. Its introduction might occur with any of the numerous plants purchased from the public nurseries. Another foreigner that has become quite established, and spreads freely, is the evening primrose *(Œnothera biennis)*, from North America. It is very plentiful, and takes possession of any piece of waste ground recently trenched or turned up. The above must be considered as only a few of the many wild plants that are to be found in the Park, commonly distributed species being withheld from these notes; while exact habitats are, for obvious reasons, suppressed. Of grasses alone, forty-seven kinds have been collected; but how many of these are not truly wild, but introduced for pasture purposes, it would be difficult to say.

BIRDS.—Amongst birds, one of the rarest visitors to the Park is the green woodpecker *(Picus viridis)*, which formerly nested in an elm tree by the Ranger's House, but which I have only twice seen since the opening up of the grounds to the public. The carrion crow *(Corvus corone)* has also ceased to breed in the Park for the same reason, though for many years the old chestnut trees by the mound were frequented by several of these birds. Being doubtful as to whether the carrion crow would breed in the Park, I pointed out the circumstance to my friend, Mr. H. E. Dresser, author of "The Birds of Europe," who has kindly assisted me in determining other species, and he said that, although unusual, it was not at all unlikely that this crow would nest in the position indicated.

Unless one is acquainted with the particular note of the kingfisher *(Alcedo ispida)*, or is attracted by its gaudy, changing colours, the bird is by no means readily detected. It often visits the pond in the Park, fishing quietly from the overhanging branches, and invariably flies off in the direction of the lake by the railway side, between Blackheath and Lewisham Stations. It does not breed in the Park, there being no banks sufficiently steep or sandy; but I have several times within an hour watched both male and female birds come to the pond to fish and fly off with their prey in the direction above mentioned, so that in all probability the breeding-ground of the kingfisher is not far from Blackheath. I have seen a nest unearthed at Keston which was simply a quantity of loosely-placed fish-bones, the stench from these being anything but pleasant. As many as four kingfishers have been seen flitting about the pond at the same time, and so tame that they frequently passed within twenty feet of workmen employed at puddling. Unfortunately, two of these birds have been killed lately—one by flying against the windows of the

FAUNA AND FLORA.

Ranger's House, and another was picked up dead in the Park, having been shot on Blackheath.

Last September a specimen of the landrail, or corncraik *(Crex pratensis)*, was found in an exhausted condition by the rock fountain. The fact of being migratory will no doubt account for the capture of this bird, and also for the emaciated condition in which it was found.

For three years at least the lesser grebe, or dabchick *(Podiceps minor)*, has reared its young on the pond, and visitors have been greatly delighted with the diving feats of this thoroughly aquatic bird and its power of remaining for so long a time beneath water when in search of food. It is migratory, and leaves about September.

The lesser grebe should not be confused with the moor or water-hen *(Gallinula chloropus)*, which is always to be found on the pond, the former having webbed feet and a duck-like head; while its diving propensities will form an unerring guide to its identity. Moorhens have increased much of late, from sixteen to twenty being frequently visible at the same time.

A pair of teal *(Anas crecca)* have more than once visited the pond in the early morning, but always make off on the appearance of visitors. This also applies to the wild duck.

Both the kestrel *(Falco tinnunculus)* and the sparrow hawk *(Accipiter nisus)* may occasionally be seen in the Park—the former frequently in the old oaks in the deer-park—but neither has nested so far as I am aware.

The common owl *(Strix flammea)* breeds annually in the Park, and in the early morning a pair may frequently be seen in the old elm trees between the Royal Observatory and Hospital. It is interesting that this owl has nested in three different parts of the Park during the past four years, and I am glad to say the young have been successfully reared. Only once have I seen the tawny owl (*Syrnium stridula*).

Jackdaws (*Corvus monedula*) are very common, and breed in the deer park; and this also applies to the wood-pigeon and ring-necked pigeon, turtle and stock doves, all of which during the spring and summer are frequently to be met with. The rock-pigeon (*Columba levis*), which Darwin mentioned as the parent of all our domesticated forms, frequently comes to the Park; but Mr. Dresser thinks it very unlikely that it would breed there. Rarely have I seen the nightjar, or goat-sucker (*Caprimulgus Europæus*); but once I watched it for a considerable time hunting for moths in the tree nursery.

With the introduction of hemp as an ornamental plant, the numbers of greenfinches (*Coccothraustes chloris*) and linnets have greatly increased, the seed being a favourite food of these birds. The goldfinch, bullfinch, siskin, house and tree sparrows, chaffinch, and redpoll have all frequently been noted — some rarely, and others, as the sparrow and chaffinch, frequently.

Three or four specimens of the crossbill (*Loxia curvirostra*), in which the mandibles of the bill are crossed for ease in extracting the pine seeds, I have seen; but their favourite food being scarce will, no doubt, account for the shortness of their visits.

The nuthatch (*Sitta Europæa*), although difficult to see, owing to its shunning the company of other birds, is quite common, and has bred in my garden. Like the woodpecker, this interesting little bird runs with ease up and down the trunk searching for insects and their *larvæ*, which form a portion of its food. Berries and nuts are, however, also eaten, and it is interesting to watch the bird fasten the nut, or acorn, in a chink of the bark, and crack it by repeated strokes of the bill.

In my own garden I once saw a flock of long-tailed tits *(Paris caudatus)*, where they remained for several hours; the common wren is plentiful, as are also the fly-catcher, redbreast, starling, and hedge-accentor. For four years past the pied wagtail *(Motacilla Yarrellii)* has reared its young by the base of an ivy-covered oak in the Park; and from the frequent visits paid by the yellow wagtail *(Motacilla flava)* to my croquet ground — often several times in an evening—I am inclined to think that it also nests in the Park. To the deer park and Ranger's grounds the cuckoo often pays a visit; but I have seen no young birds. The sedge-warbler has also been observed; and on several occasions I have seen the stonechat flying about in the deer enclosure. Swallows breed annually in the old barn and deer-sheds, but the swift and sand-martin can only be recorded as occasional visitors.

The blackbird, song-thrush, and missel-thrush all breed regularly, the latter having for three successive seasons reared its young in the paddock attached to the deer park. Once, and only once, have I seen the lark alight in the Park, and once the hawfinch and nightingale.

Four species of tit—the great tit, blue tit, marsh tit, and long-tailed tit—are not at all uncommon, the two former having nested near the Blackheath entrance last spring. The golden-crested wren *(Rigulus cristatus)* I have seen more than once. Two specimens of the quail were found in the Park lately; and Mr. Russell, of Vanbrugh Fields, tells me that he has seen the woodcock and partridge in the Park.

ANIMALS.—As might be expected, animals are not abundant in the Park, this being due in great measure to the high wall with which it is surrounded.

The rabbit, rat, watervole, dormouse, shrew, and fieldmouse are abundant; while the bat is to be seen at any time during not too severe weather.

The long-eared bat breeds regularly in a hollow oak in the deer-park, and the vole, or short-tailed water-rat, occasionally puts in an appearance. Hedgehogs have been introduced. Both a fox and hare have visited the Park.

FISH comprise the carp, perch, pike, roach, goldfish (introduced), and stickle-back. The frog, toad, common and warty newt are abundant.

When the small acreage and unfavourable surroundings are taken into account, it will be admitted that the Flora and Fauna of the Park are extremely varied and interesting. I have no hesitation, however, in saying that were it not for the enclosed portions of the Park — the Wilderness, Ranger's ground, Observatory, One Tree Hill, and deer enclosure — many of the birds which now breed and find a home would only be known as casual visitors, and the rarer plants would cease to exist.

The following is a complete list of the birds and plants that I have observed in the Park:—

BIRDS.

Kestrel
Sparrowhawk
*Barn owl
Tawny owl
*Spotted flycatcher
*Missel thrush
Fieldfare
*Song thrush
Redwing
*Blackbird
*Hedge accentor
*Redbreast
Redstart

Stonechat
Whinchat
*Sedge warbler
*Reed warbler
Nightingale
*Blackcap
Garden warbler
*Whitethroat
Woodwren
Willow warbler
Chiff-chaff
Golden-crested regulus
*Great tit

Those marked with an asterisk (*) breed in the Park.

FAUNA AND FLORA. 51

*Blue tit
*Cole tit
Marsh tit
Longtailed tit
*Pied wagtail
Grey wagtail
Rays wagtail
Tree pipit
Skylark
*Common bunting
Yellow bunting
Tree sparrow
Quail
Partridge
*House sparrow
*Greenfinch
Hawfinch
Goldfinch
Siskin
*Linnet
Lesser redpoll
*Bullfinch
Crossbill
*Starling
*Carrion crow
Hooded crow
*Jackdaw
Rook

*Green woodpecker
Lesser spotted woodpecker
Wryneck
*Creeper
*Wren
*Nuthatch
Cuckoo
Kingfisher
*Swallow
Martin
Sand martin
Swift
Nightjar
*Ringdove
*Stockdove
*Turtledove
*Pigeon
Landrail
*Moorhen
Wild duck
Teal
*Lesser grebe
Sea gull
Black-backed gull
Woodcock
Peewit
Golden plover

Those marked with an asterisk (*) breed in the Park.

PLANTS.

Acer campestre
Achillea millæfolium
Aconitum napellus
Agremonia upatoria
Agrostemma Githago
Aira cæspitosa
Aira flexuosa
Alisma natans
Alisma plantago
Alnus glutinosa
Alopecurus pratensis
Anemone nemorosa
Antennaria dioica

Aquilegia vulgaris
Arenaria peploides
Armeria vulgaris
Arum maculatum
Arundo phragmites
Aspidium filix-mas
Atriplex hortensis
Avena pratensis
Bellis perennis
Berberis vulgaris
Bromus arvensis
Bromus giganteus
Butomus umbellatus

Calamintha officinalis
Caltha palustris
Campanula glomerata
Campanula rapunculoides
Campanula rotundifolia
Campanula trachelium
Carduus acaulis
Carex (many species)
Centaurea cyanus
Ceterach officinarum
Chlora perfoliata
Chrysanthemum
           leucanthemum
Circea lutetiana
Claytonia perfoliata
Clematis vitalba
Colchicum autumnale
Convolvulus arvensis
Cornus sanguinea
Cratægus oxyacantha
Crocus nudiflorus
Cuscuta europea
Cynoglossum officinale
Cytisus scoparius
Dactylis glomerata
Daphne mezereum
Datura stramonium
Daucas carota
Digitalis purpurea
Dipsacus fullonium
Dipsacus sylvestris
Draba muralis
Echium vulgare
Elodea canadensis
Elymus arenarius
Epilobium (several species)
Equisetum arvense
Erica vulgaris
Euphorbia æsula
Euonymus europœus
Fagus sylvatica
Fœniculum vulgaris
Fraxinus excelsior
Galanthus nivalis
Geranium sylvaticum
Hedera helix

Helianthemum vulgare
Heracleum sphondylium
Holcus mollis
Hordeum pratense
Hordeum sylvaticum
Hottonia palustris
Humulus lupulus
Hydrocharis morsus-ranœ
Hyoscyamus niger
Hypericum androsæmum
Hypericum calycinum
Hypericum humifusum
Hypericum perforatum
Ilex aquifolium
Iris pseud-acorus
Lactuca muralis
Lamium album
Lathyrus sylvestris
Ligustrum vulgare
Linaria cymbalaria
Lychnis vespertina
Lysimachia nummularia
Lythrum salicaria
Malva sylvestris
Mentha aquatica
Mentha sylvestris
Menyanthes trifoliata
Mercurialis annua
Mespilus germanica
Myosotis sylvatica
Narcissus pseudo-narciss
Nuphar lutea
Nymphea alba
Œnothera biennis
Orobanche minor
Oxalis acetosella
Oxalis corniculata
Papaver rhœas
Phleum pratense
Pinus sylvestris
Plantago major
Poa annua
Poa aquatica
Poa fluitans
Poa trivialis
Polygonatum multiflorum

Polygonum bistorta
Polygonum viviparum
Polypodium vulgare
Populus alba
Potamogeton crispus
Potamogeton perfoliatus
Potentilla argentea
Primula veris
Primula vulgaris
Prunus Padus
Pteris aquilina
Pyrus aria
Pyrus torminalis
Quercus robur
Ranunculus aquatilis
Ribes grossularia
Rosa canina
Rubus fruticosus
Rumex acetosella
Rumex sanguineus
Ruscus aculeatus
Sagittaria sagittifolia
Salix alba
Sambucus nigra
Samolas valerandi
Scabiosa arvensis
Scilla nutans
Scilla autumnalis (introduced)
Scolopendrium vulgare
Sedum acre
Silene armeria
Silene inflata
Silene nutans
Solanum dulcamara
Solanum nigra
Sparganium ramosum
Spirea ulmaria
Stellaria (several species)
Trogopogon porrifolius
Tamus communis
Tussilago farfara
Typha angustifolia
Typha latifolia
Ulex europœus
Ulmus montana
Urtica dioica
Valeriana officinalis
Verbascum blattaria
Verbascum nigrum
Verbascum thapsus
Veronica beccabunga
Veronica spicata
Viola tricolor
Vicia sativa
Vicia sepium
Vicia sylvaticum
Vicia tetrasperma

Trees and Shrubs in Greenwich Park.

Perhaps no other Park around London can approach Greenwich, either for the number and size of its Spanish chestnuts, or the variety of its flowering trees and shrubs. For purely educational purposes, the collection of trees, shrubs, and other plants is extremely valuable; a large number of schools in which botany is taught, being now supplied with specimens from the Park. But this is not all, as the labelling of the plants with their popular and scientific names, has borne excellent results, by disseminating a knowledge and extending the culture of the best kinds for decorative purposes. Amongst forest trees, the Spanish chestnuts, already referred to, have attained unusual proportions, the gravelly soil of the Park being peculiarly suitable for their growth and perfect development, while the elm and oak have done fairly well. Many of these old trees are, however, in a rapidly declining condition, whether owing to old age, or the result of accidents to their leaders and branches during stormy weather. This is, especially, the case with the older elms, the majority of which have become diseased and rotten at the core, by the ingress of water from the point where a branch had become broken off by the force of the wind.

It may not be generally known that one of the largest thorns in this country is growing in the grounds of the Ranger's Lodge, a little distance from the Blackheath entrance. It is fully 50 feet high, and over 7 feet in girth of stem. The chestnut-leaved oak *(Quercus castanæfolia)* has a noble representative near the old bath; while the purple-leaved beech, whose branch spread is 57 feet in diameter, has few equals around London. Other interesting trees in the same grounds, are the tulip tree, with a fine clean bole 60 feet in height; the ailanthus or tree of Heaven; the yellow-flowered horse chestnut, and a giant specimen of the medlar, all of which are growing around what is known as "The Mound." Nearer to the Ranger's Lodge, is a goodly specimen of that, by no means common Canadian tree, the june berry *(Amelanchier)*; though of the same species, an almost unique representative may be seen in one of the tree-clumps on the left of the main avenue, about midway between Blackheath entrance and the Royal Observatory. Other rare

Photo by Mr. Potter.

OLD SPANISH CHESTNUT IN GREENWICH PARK.

trees and shrubs in the Ranger's Grounds, are the golden catalpa, cut-leaved beam, several specimens of the snowdrop tree *(Halesia tetraptera)*, Pyrus torminalis, as well as a rich collection of hardy heaths, azaleas, rhododendrons, ralmias, and the far from common lily of the valley tree *(Andromeda cassinæfolia)*, many fine plants of which are to be found in the dell. There is also a well shaped and healthy specimen of the hornbeam by the fence opposite the Ranger's House, while the London plane, and several forms of acacia are quite at home amongst the smoke and soot to which the Park every day is becoming more subjected. Both the holly and evergreen oak have attained unusual dimensions. But by far the richest collection of shrubs and trees in the Park, is in the enclosed ground by the pond, where not less than 1,300 kinds are to be seen. Here are magnolias, ornamental thorns, arbutus, almonds, paper birch, double flowering cherrys, berberis, the beautiful flowering viburnum plicatum, buddleas, ceonathus in variety, dogwoods, and hosts of other rare and interesting trees and shrubs. Amongst the rarer shrubs, special mention may be made of the far from common Clerodendron trichotomum, which is growing in the hollow near the pond, the curious colluteas and Dutchman's pipe, the Paliurus, or Christ's thorn, Californian myrtle, and poison ivy *(Rhus toxicodendron)*, the foliage of which latter passes into the deepest crimson with the approach of winter, the Mexican orange flower *(Choisya)*, and the interesting and free-flowering hydrangeas. Many forms of bramble do well, but particularly the double-flowering variety of our native plant. Bamboos do remarkably well, as several large beds will bear testimony; the most suitable kinds being the best known Bambusa Metake, the graceful B. nigra, palmata, Simoni, and aurea. The big clumps of

Zebra grass *(Eulalia zebrina),* are particularly handsome from August onwards, while the pampas grass throws its silky heads to fully 6 feet in height.

Roses, particularly species, do well in the Park, and the handsome plant of R. Wichuriana, which covers part of the sloping ground by the pond, when wreathed in its pure white, deliciously fragrant flowers, has few equals as a screen plant; other interesting species are R. pomifera, which bears fruit like small pinky-cheeked apples; the Japanese R. rugosa, both white and pink; the prairie and Abyssinian roses. The crimson rambler, too, is well suited for cultivation in the Park, where it grows freely and bears flowers in the richest abundance; what may also be said of Lord Penzance's sweet briars, which may be classed as amongst the most useful for wild gardening. The Hibiscus does remarkably well in the Park, the finest specimen being in the grounds of the Royal Observatory; while the arbutus, or strawberry tree, in the shrubbery around the Kent Water Works Reservoir, has attained to a goodly size.

Aquatic plants are well represented in the pond, some of the rarer water lilies having become quite established, and flower freely from year to year. The continental pink and rosy flowered varieties, though sadly handicapped by the American weed, are flourishing and increasing, as the large, well formed flowers would indicate. The sweetly scented Cape pond weed *(Aponogeton)* has also done well, and produces in abundance its curiously shaped and deliciously fragrant flowers. Other interesting aquatic plants are the native bogbean, of which large masses may be noticed; the water plantain, the greater and lesser bulrushes *(Typha)*, which revel by the water side, and the curious water soldier *(Stratiotes aloides).*

PARK.

Photo by Mr. Potter.

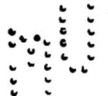

TREES AND SHRUBS. 57

Of Semi-Aquatic plants, the Royal fern *(Osmunda)* attains to goodly proportions; while the mocassin flower *(Cypripedium spectabile)* from North America, and the Maderia orchid *(Orchis foliosa)*, have both become established, and produce in abundance their quaintly-shaped flowers. The lyme-grass has a pretty effect by the water margin, in consequence of the deep blue metallic leaves, a worthy companion being found in the great reed *(Arando donax)*, which rises to fully 6 feet in height.

Gunnera manicata, with its immense rhubarb-like leaves and curious flower spike, has attracted considerable notice during the past season, it being a plant of noble growth, and peculiarly suitable for well-chosen spots by the water side. The New Zealand flax and Japanese polygonum are other attractive plants for growing in suitable spots near water.

But we must not omit to make mention of the noble Eryngium Pandanifolium, which, in one of the wild beds, sends up its handsome flower-spike to the height of a man, the deep green aloe-like foliage, rendering it one of the best subjects for ornamental gardening.

Bulbous plants have been largely made use of of late years, particularly amongst the grass, and on examination of any of the enclosed grounds during early spring, will clearly demonstrate that such a method of planting has many points in its favour. Narcissus of many kinds, tulips, snowdrops, Winter aconite, crocus, squills, and the lovely glory of the snow *(Chionodoxa)*, have all been treated in this way, by planting in big irregular masses. The best daffodils for naturalising in the Park are Sir Watkin, the pheasant's eye, telamonius plenus, maximus, and the Lent lily — pseudo-Narcissus, although the Tenby *(Obvallaris)* and jonquil are not to be despised.

Except in the borders by the entrance gates, the "bedding out" system is entirely dispensed with, the beautifully undulating and well wooded character of the grounds being far too natural to admit of such a system—indeed, in the management of the Park, one of the principal objects aimed at has been to cherish and retain, as far as possible, the wild and natural character of this royal heritage.

Entomology of the Park.

When we take into consideration the small acreage of Greenwich Park, its proximity to the great Metropolis, and environs of bricks and mortar, it is truly surprising the variety of insect life that is to be met with; and we may well feel proud that such noble moths as the "death's head," "goat," and "leopard" are still to be numbered amongst those which are found in fair abundance. The insect life of the Park suffers from at least three disadvantages—proximity to the smoke of London, the teeming population, and insufficient undergrowth. On the other hand, the warm gravelly and sandy soils are distinct advantages, while the old and decaying trees afford excellent quarters for a teeming host of such insect life as is generally termed injurious to forest trees, and which passes the greater part of its existence in decayed and decaying wood. The older Spanish chestnut trees are in some instances literally tunnelled by the caterpillar of the beautiful wood leopard moth (*Zeuzera æsculi*), while the elms readily fall a prey to the goat moth (*Cossus ligniperda*), and the elm bark beetle (*Scolytus destructor*), both of which are very abundant in the Park. Of foliage-destroying insects, the oak leaf roller moth (*Tortrix viridana*) and the holy fly *(Phytomyza aquifolia)* are to be found in fair abundance, the relative scarcity of oaks helping to keep the former in check. The following list has been kindly compiled for me by Stanley Edwards, Esq,. F.R.G.S., F.L.S., F.Z.S., of Kidbrook Lodge, Blackheath:

RHAPALOCERA, OR BUTTERFLIES OF GREENWICH PARK.

Pieris	Urticae	Pamphilus
Brassicæ	Polychloros	Thecla
Rapae	Io	Rubi
Napi	Atalanta	Polyommatus
Anthocharis	Cardui	Phlæas
Curdamines	Satyrus	Lycæna
Gonepteryx	Ianira	Argiolus
Rhamni	Tithonus	Alexis
Vanessa	Chortobius	

HETEROCERA, OR MOTHS OF GREENWICH PARK.

Smerinthus	Hectus	Antiqua
Ocellatus	Lupulinus	Pœcilocampa
Populi	Sylvinus	Populi
Tiliae	Humuli	Bombyx
Acherontia	Nola	Neustria
Atropos	Cucullatella	Odonestis
Sphinx	Lithosia	Potatoria
Colvolvuli	Complanula	Urapteryx
Ligustri	Chelonia	Sambucata
Macroglossa	Caja	Epione
Stellatarum	Arctia	Rumia
Sesia	Lubricipeda	Crataegata
Tipuliformis	Menthastri	Metrocampa
Culiciformis	Liparis	Margaritaria
Zenzera	Chrysorrhæa	Selenia
Æsculi	Auriflua	Lunaria
Cossus	Salicis	Odontopera
Ligniperda	Orgyia	Bidentata
Hepialus	Pudibunda	Crocallis

Elinguaria
Ennomos
Tiliaria
Himera
Pennaria
Phigalia
Pilosaria
Biston
Hirtaria
Amphidasis
Prodromaria
Betularia
Hemerophila
Abruptaria
Boarmia
Repandara
Rhomboidaria
Iodis
Vernaria
Lactearia
Hemithea
Thymiaria
Acidalia
Scutulata
Bisetata
Incanaria
Remutata
Imitaria
Aversata
Cabera
Pusaria
Halia
Wavaria
Panagra
Petraria
Numeria
Pulveraria
Abrascas
Grossulariata
Hybernia
Progemmaria
Defoliaria
Leucophearia
Anisopteryx
Æscularia
Cheimatobia

Brun'ata
Oporabia
Dilutata
Eupithecia
Vulgata
Rectangulata and
 var. nigrosericeata
centaureata
Castigata
Pumilata
Thera
Variata
Hypsipetes
Elutata
Melanippe
Tristata
Fluctuata
Anticlea
Badiata
Camptogramma
Bilineata
Phibalapteryx
Tersata
Scotosia
Rhamnata
Certata
Cidaria
Populata
Fulvata
Dotata
Pelurga
Comitata
Eubolia
Mensuraria
Anaitis
Plagiata
Platypheryx
Lacertula
Falcula
Cilix
Spinula
Dicranura
Bifida
Vinula
Pygaera
Bucephala

Ptilodontis
Palpina
Notodonta
Camelina
Diloba
Cæruleocephala
Thyatira
Botis
Derasa
Cymatophora
Diluta
Bryophila
Perla
Acronycta
Psi
Tridens
Megacephala
Leucania
Lithargyria
Comma
Pallens
Hydræcia
Nictitans
Axylia
Putris
Xylophasia
Lithoxylea
Rurea
Polyodon
Dipterygia
Pinastri
Heliophobus
Popularis
Cerigo
Cytherea
Luperina
Testacea
Mamestra
Brassicae
Persicariae
Apamea
Basilinea
Ophiogramma
Oculea
Miana
Strigilis

FUNGI. 61.

Arcuosa	Cruda	Aprilina
Fasciuncula	Gracilis	Phlogaphora
Caradrina	Munda	Meticulosa
Morpheus	Orthosia	Euplexia
Blanda	Lota	Lucipara
Cubicularis	Macilenta	Aplecta
Rusina	Anchocelis	Nebulosa
Tenebrosa	Rufina	Hadena
Agrotis	Pistacina	Dentina
Puta	Litura	Chenopodii
Suffusa	Cerastis	Oleracea
Segetum	Vaccinii	Xylocampa
Exclamationis	Spadicea	Lithoriza
Saucia	Scopelosoma	Calocampa
Triphæna	Satellitia	Vetusta
Janthina	Xanthia	Exoleta
Fimbria	Citrago	Cucullia
Orbona	Cerago	Chamomillae
Pronuba	Ferruginea	Plusia
Noctua	Cosmia	Chrysitis
Augur	Trapezina	Gamma
Plecta	Pyralina	Gonoptera
C. nigrum	Diffinis	Libatrix
Festiva	Dianthœcia	Amphipyra
Baja	Carpophaga	Tragopogonis
Xanthographa	Hecatera	Mania
Taeniocampa	Serena	Typica
Gothica	Miselia	Maura
Instabilis	Oxyacanthæ	Catocola
Stabilis	Agriopis	Nupta

FUNGI OF GREENWICH PARK.

Perhaps it is nothing to be proud of, but Greenwich Park can boast of an unusually large collection of toadstools, ranging from the giant rugged tenant of the decaying elm, which may often be met with 18 inches in diameter, to the pretty tinted cups of several minute forms of Peziza. For centuries, both far and near, the Park has been known as the home of the edible "Champignon" (*Marasmius oreades*); and during the spring and summer months, as soon as the Park gates are opened, numbers of persons may be seen searching amongst the grass for this toothsome member of the great fungus family. The common and horse mushrooms (*Agaricus campestris* and *A. arvensis*) are, likewise, abundant, particularly in flower borders that have been enriched with the manure and sweepings of the Greenwich streets. Amongst other edible fungi that I have come across are the "Blewits" (*Tricholoma personata*), with its purple-tinged stem; the oyster mushroom (*Pleurotus ostreatus*), the mouse-coloured cups of which may often be seen in dense tufts around decaying tree stumps; the vegetable beefsteak (*Fistulina hepatica*), and the inky mushroom (*Coprinus atramentarius*), which, though edible in a young state, has a disagreeable appearance when melting away like ink after perfect development. Another edible kind common in the Park is that known as the "Horn of Plenty" (*Craterellus cornucopioides*), with its curious dark grey trumpet-shaped cups.

Poisonous species have a wide range, and would include the "Stinking Amanita" (*Amanita phalloidea*), which is found in the deer park; the warm, tan-coloured *Lepiota granulosa*, the beautiful golden-tinted *Pholiota spectabilis*, the jelly-like *Tremella foliacea*, and the well known "Stinkhorn" (*Phallus impudicus*).

These are only a few of the many Fungi that are to be found in the Park, particularly the private portions of the Observatory and One Tree Hills, the deer park, pond, and Ranger's enclosures. The old oaks, elms, and Spanish chestnuts, when decayed, afford excellent hosts for several species, and the enormous size to which some of these attain has often been the source of discussion; indeed, Greenwich Park may be classed as one of the few happy hunting grounds for Fungi that now exist in the great Metropolis.

Notes on the Geology of Greenwich Park.

By T. V. Holmes, Esq., F.G.S.

The oldest formation visible within a radius of many miles around Greenwich is the Chalk. But nowhere does it form part of the surface of Greenwich Park, though it lies beneath the old river gravel which covers the low ground between the northern boundary and the base of the slopes bounding the plateau on the edge of which the Observatory stands. North of a line which nearly coincides with the northern boundary of the Park, a "fault," or dislocation of the strata, throws down the Chalk, with the Tertiary beds overlying it. In consequence of the existence of this "fault," a well south of it, at the Greenwich Union Infirmary, showed Chalk at 30ft. from the surface, covered only by old river gravel, formed when the Thames flowed at a slightly higher level than at present. At Greenwich Hospital Brewery, north of the "fault," the top of the Chalk was reached at a depth of 124ft. 6in. Above it were, in ascending order, the Thanet sand, Woolwich beds, and Blackheath pebble beds, which form the higher ground in the Park, in addition to the old river gravel which extends thence to the Thames unaffected by the "fault."

The oldest of the Tertiary beds which rest upon the Chalk is the light-coloured sand which is shown in the railway cutting between Maze Hill and Westcombe Park Railway Stations, and in the pit at the foot of Maze Hill in the Park itself. Its thickness hereabouts is from 40ft. to 50ft. It forms the lower part of the slopes which bound the plateau formed by the higher part of the Park and Blackheath. Above this sand, known geologically as the Thanet sand, come the Woolwich beds, which consist of a very variable series of bands of sand, loam, pebbles, and clay. The most interesting and important member of this series is a clayey bed containing many shells, now well shown in the railway cutting east of Blackheath Station, at the junction of the Bexley Heath and Charlton lines. The total thickness of the Woolwich beds in the Park is, probably, about 20ft., and they occupy the middle of the slopes. Above them, capping the plateau, are the Blackheath pebble beds, which have been much worked for gravel, both on Blackheath and in the higher part of Greenwich Park. Their thickness is, probably, 40ft., or more. For there are gravel pits on Blackheath, near the south-eastern corner of the Park, attaining a depth of about 30ft., yet which show no permanent wetness at the bottom. And when an attempt was made, in 1881, to explore the subsidence which occurred on Blackheath, near the road on the western side of the Ride, water was first encountered at a depth of 34ft. This marked the level, in a dry season, of the water which, percolating through the Blackheath pebble beds as rain, is prevented from descending lower by the presence of the clayey shell beds of the Woolwich series.

It may be worth while noting here that in shallow ponds, like that in the Park, the water is kept from sinking lower by the soil and mud washed into them, which make an impermeable lining.

The scenery of this Lower Tertiary ridge, or escarpment, which crosses the Park, but ranges from Blackheath Hill to Erith, is much influenced by the presence of the impermeable bands of the Woolwich series. For the rain falling on the Blackheath pebble beds capping the plateau, of which the Lower Tertiary escarpment is the northern outcrop and boundary, tends to come out in the form of springs towards the bottom of the pebble beds. Some minute local peculiarity determines the exact spot at which a spring begins to flow. Once started, the influence of the spring is in aid of the various denuding agencies at that spot, and causes the ridge to be eroded back there more rapidly than elsewhere. In this way have been evolved the numerous combes, or sinuous hollows in the face of the Lower Tertiary escarpment between the Ravensbourne and the Darent. West of the Park is that of Hyde Vale. Within the Park are one on the west side of Observatory Hill, and another on the east. On the west a branch of the combe winds eastward into the Observatory garden, thereby giving a stronger natural site to the Castle which preceded the Observatory. East of the Observatory, and between it and One Tree Hill, there is a more extensive combe, with many ramifications east and west of the broad walk ascending its slope. Beyond the Park, eastward, the names Westcombe and East-combe tell their own tale.

Ridges of gravel, sand, and clay, like that crossing Greenwich Park, tend always to have the nature of their real constituents obscured by the fall of material down the slopes from the upper on to the lower beds. In Greenwich Park, the Blackheath pebble beds have been much washed down by rain. In times quite recent, this has been very conspicuous whenever and wherever the brow of the ridge has been allowed to become bare of grass or other green covering. On this account the slopes appear to consist wholly of gravel, instead of the various beds which would be exposed by a deep cutting into the hillside.

Some care is necessary in distinguishing between the natural and artificial features of the ground in the Park. In the upper part, banks steeper than usual are very frequently the result of old diggings for gravel at that spot, now smooth and covered with grass. In the lower part of the Park there has been much artificial terracing, dating from the 17th century, having the Queen's House as its centre. The visitor who has not been in the habit of studying surface features should always bear in mind the fact that Nature abhors straight lines and right angles, and delights in easy and graceful curves.

In conclusion, it may be of interest to note that as Greenwich Park owes its existence to the prior existence of Greenwich Palace, so the Palace was built where it once stood, because on its site, and that of the town of Greenwich generally, there is a bed of old river gravel close to the Thames, and yet above the reach of floods. Proximity to that great highway, combined with a sufficiently elevated gravelly, or sandy site, made a spot specially attractive as a centre for population in the olden time. For from the lower part of the gravel a water supply was obtainable by means of pumps and shallow wells. In the site of the old City of London, we have a spot even more attractive than that of Greenwich, from the presence there of a much larger spread of old river gravel, at a greater elevation, yet equally near the Thames.

by Sturdee.

Roman Remains in Greenwich Park.

Although Greenwich cannot claim to be one of the great centres of Roman discovery, yet a complete list of the places in its immediate vicinity where Roman remains have been brought to light would be rather a lengthy one.

In addition to the important finds at Keston and Dartford, and the well-known Watling Street, or Roman road from London to Dover—which, by the way, passed through Greenwich—remains have been found at Blackheath and Croydon, some of which would probably carry us back even further than the time of the Romans.

However that may be, the Greenwich Park discovery is important, adding as it does another link to the chain of evidence respecting the Roman occupation of this part of the County, and surpassing in interest any previously recorded from the immediate neighbourhood.

As already stated, there were, however, other evidences of a less distinct character of the presence of the Romans near Greenwich, for we find that in 1803 several Roman urns were discovered by some labourers when digging in the kitchen garden of Dartmouth House, Blackheath. They contained fragments of bone imperfectly burnt, and are now deposited in the British Museum. At Westcombe Park Roman remains have also been discovered; while between the Park boundary and river several indications of Roman occupation have lately come to light, including tessellated pavement, a Roman medal, and a fasces, an axe bound with a bundle of rods, which was carried by each of the twelve lictors, who preceded the chief magistrate, as a symbol of authority. In 1710, several urns were found on

Blackheath, one bearing the inscription "Marcvs Aurelivs IV.," and another contained two coins of Claudius and Gallienius.

But notwithstanding these minor indications of the Romans in the neighbourhood, the discovery at Greenwich Park must be regarded as essentially new, the existence of a villa in the Park not being included on any plan of the Roman roads, nor on the maps of the Ordnance Survey. The discovery came about in a simple way, and would in all probability have been made some time before had a suitable opportunity occurred. When trying to locate the position of several barrows, and the site of Watling Street, the mound on which the remains have been found was, along with several others, mapped out as likely to afford traces which would be a guide to further observation and research. Unfortunately, an opportunity did not occur until the beginning of the present year (6th February), when, on working at one of the conduits close by, a search was made in the mound by probing the soil with an iron bar. As a result several tesseræ and cement were discovered, which at once confirmed the existence of Roman remains. The matter was communicated to Herbert Jones, Esq., F.L.S., F.S.A., to whom we are greatly indebted for valuable assistance during the excavations, and under whose guidance a trench was cut through the mound, when the remains of a floor to a length of about 18ft. were laid bare, and a large quantity of tesseræ, wall plaster (coloured and plain), roofing and other tiles, as also a Roman coin, were discovered, thus lending encouragement for future investigation.

Further search was made on the 3rd March, when the floor of a room with a portion of the tesseræ intact was happily hit upon at a distance from the surface of hardly 2ft. A quantity of coloured wall plaster, roofing and other tiles, nails, and a number of coins were likewise found. This portion has been left uncovered, and fenced around to prevent damage, and in order that the public might have an opportunity of viewing these interesting and historic remains. Still further search on the 17th and 18th of the month disclosed a number of levelled walls, several coins, an inscription on marble, and quantities of broken pottery of no fewer than about thirteen distinct kinds. Some pieces of Samian ware were beautifully decorated, although much that was plain, and others in imitation, were likewise found. Black pottery was found in great abundance, particularly in refuse pits; also the neck of an amphora, and several jugs, pieces of iron and bronze, a key, blade of a knife, and large numbers of nails and spikes; but as these are referred to in a separate list, they need not receive special attention here.

It is most unfortunate that, although numerous indications of concrete and other flooring were unearthed, the walls had in all cases been cleared away, leaving little of their previous existence *in situ*—in fact, the whole buildings would appear to have been demolished in a wholesale and ruthless manner. This is, perhaps, not difficult to account for, the absence of stone quarries around Blackheath and Greenwich, from which building materials could be procured, furnishing us with a clue as to how the stones of the villa were utilised for house building at a later date.

Be this as it may, no clear indications of walls in their original positions have been found, although in several instances fallen walls with tiles mortared to the stones were discovered in the course of excavation. That walls of a costly character were connected with the villa, the numerous remains of beautifully designed and coloured plaster, of which about a dozen distinct patterns have been found, show; while the unusually heavy roofing tiles and worked oolite slabs tell that the building was of a very substantial nature.

The pavement, which has been fenced around for examination, was found comparatively near the surface, the depth of soil hardly exceeding 8 to 10 inches. It was quite unprotected, and had evidently been much broken and disturbed when the circle of elm trees, which cap the mound on which the discovery was made, were planted some 250 years ago; indeed, the existing portion escaped mainly owing to its proximity to the boundary wall of the building. The concrete foundation on which the tesseræ rest is of rather a formidable nature, averaging 9 inches in depth, and is remarkably hard and well preserved. There does not appear to have been a hypocaust under this pavement, although traces of such with round tiles were found on a slightly lower level at no great distance away.

Judging from the large quantity of ashes, charcoal, nails with burnt wood attached, and burned pottery which were found covering a considerable space on one of the floors, it would appear that a portion of the villa had been destroyed by fire. That the fire was of considerable proportions and the heat intense, is inferred from the ruined floor, and condition of the stones, which were much discoloured and cracked, as would be the case when subjected to great heat. Two coins of Hadrian were found on the burnt floor, and quantities of broken and burnt black pottery, with a large number of nails and spikes, to which, in many instances, charred wood was attached. That another building took the place of that consumed by fire is evident from the portions of a nicely executed floor which were found contiguous to and

Photo by Mr. J. P. B. Webster.

ROMAN PAVEMENT FOUND IN GREENWICH PARK.

at a higher level than that on which the charred materials were deposited, as also from built stone foundations which were come across beneath this floor and on the same level as that on which the evidences of burning were discovered.

The large number of coins that have been found —over 300—has excited a good deal of comment as to how they got deposited, as, on comparison with those unearthed at other Roman villas, the Greenwich Park number is far in excess. The site may have been a pay place for soldiers, a canteen, or the residence of an officer connected with the Mint; however, the fact of the coins being found singly over an area of nearly an acre of ground, and not contained in a pot, or urn, would point to the fact of their having been lost at various periods, as indicated by the date of the coins. It is difficult to account for the numbers of barbarous British imitations of Roman coins that were found.

Classified list of the principal objects found:—

COINS.—Coins of silver and bronze, the period ranging from B.C. 35 to A.D. 423. These are included in separate list. (One of the coins is probably unique.)

GLASS. — Several specimens of glass manufacture, including the broken handle of a jug, and many pieces beautifully frosted and coloured.

Beads round and oblong.

FLINT AND STONE. — Arm of woman supporting dress, life size, beautifully carved. Portion of statue.

Portion of a large vessel of foreign stone.

A mould cut out of chalk.

Blocks of squared stone, some roughly channelled.

Portion of inscription carved on white marble, the letters, which are an inch in length, being beautifully cut. This was found in three parts, which have been joined together, and is of particular interest as Roman inscriptions have rarely been found in southern England.

Two other carvings on rough marble, one with larger letters than above.

Inscription on sandstone.

A small number of pennant roofing tiles.

Several stones of oolite, Kentish rag, &c., bearing masons' marks.

Two whetstones.

A small series of flint chippings.

Flint core from which implements were chipped.

Small carved stone set in bronze for scarf-pin.

POTTERY.—A great quantity of broken pottery, comprising Samian, both plain and figured; imitation Samian, Salopian, Upchurch, and Castor. These were principally found in two rubbish heaps which were discovered in course of excavation.

Portions of an amphora, and mortaria.

Head of lion in terra-cotta, with nail driven through open mouth, evidently used as a charm.

Vessels of many kinds are represented by broken pottery, handles, rim mouldings, dish-covers, and ornamented stands. The vessels have been of many sizes—large and small, deep and shallow—some of rough plain pottery, and others indicate refinement from the figures and ornament. That of the Samian ware is well executed in figures of men, trees, and dogs.

Two pieces of early British pottery (a valuable find).

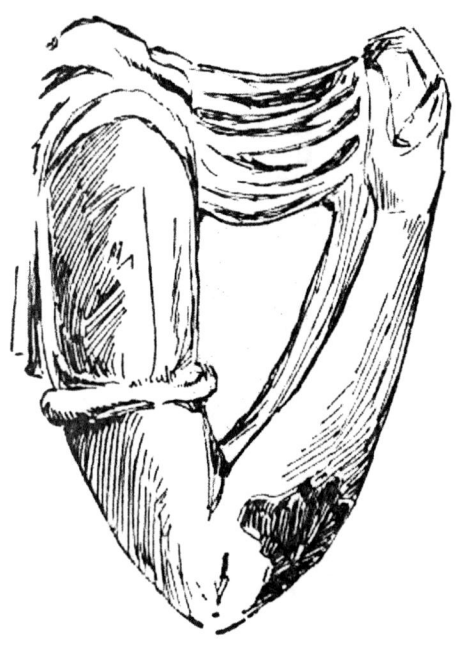

ARM OF STATUE.

ANIMAL FOOTPRINTS ON

INSCRIPTION ON SANDSTONE.

INSCRIPTION ON M

From "Daily Graphic."

FROM THE ROMAN VILLA.

Sketched by Miss A. Airy.

1.—BLACK OR POT WARE.   2, 3, 4, 7 & 8.—SAMIAN WARE.
5 & 6.—NECKS OF JARS.

ROMAN REMAINS. 73

IVORY AND BONE.—A small piece of ivory with carving of woman holding shield above her head—nicely executed.

The carved side of a box.

Knitting needle and pin.

Ivory veneers.

BRONZE.—Chain work. Part of fibula.

Small pair of neatly finished box hinges with holes for rivets.

Box or other ornament.

Eyeglass rim.

Nail cleaner.

Triangular piece of bronze—probably part of a lock.

Bronze ornamentation with small holes.

Bronze dress-fastener.

IRON.—A large number of nails and spikes, from 2 inches to 6 inches long.

Key 7 inches long, in good condition.

Knife, or chopper, with circular handle 5 inches long.

Hippo sandal.

Needle, or probe, 6 inches long.

Staples of various designs.

Ferrule, ½ inch in diameter.

Steel ring.

Part of a riding spur.

Iron hooks of various sizes.

Clamps, several.

BONES, TEETH, AND ANTLERS.—Generally speaking, these are of domesticated animals—horse, sheep, oxen, deer, &c.

Antler of red deer in good preservation, and of unusually large size. Evidently from the saw-marks where portions of the tangs had been removed, the horns were used for making knife handles and bone implements.

Antlers of fallow deer.

Bones of the ox and sheep in abundance, showing, in some instances, traces of gnawing.

Teeth—indentified as those of the horse, camel, small ox, rabbit and dog.

SHELLS.—Oyster shells in abundance were found all over the ground, but principally in the two rubbish heaps where the broken pottery was discovered in such quantity.

Shells of mussels, common and edible snails.

CHARCOAL.—In three positions remains of fires were come across, and charcoal and burnt stones found together. At the corner of a fallen wall indications of a large fire, with a layer of charcoal and ashes about a quarter of an inch in thickness, spread regularly over a surface of about two by three yards.

WALL STUCCO.—There was a large quantity of wall plaster found all over the site, but particularly by the floor with tesseræ intact. Many of the specimens retain the original colouring in a perfect condition.

The coloured figures, dadoes, borders, and floral patterns all denote that the rooms were beautifully decorated, and of more than ordinary importance. Of self colours there are bright and dark red, black, white, yellow, purple, and dark chocolate; while a white pattern will have a red dado, and a red coloured figure in white,

FROM THE ROMAN VILLA.

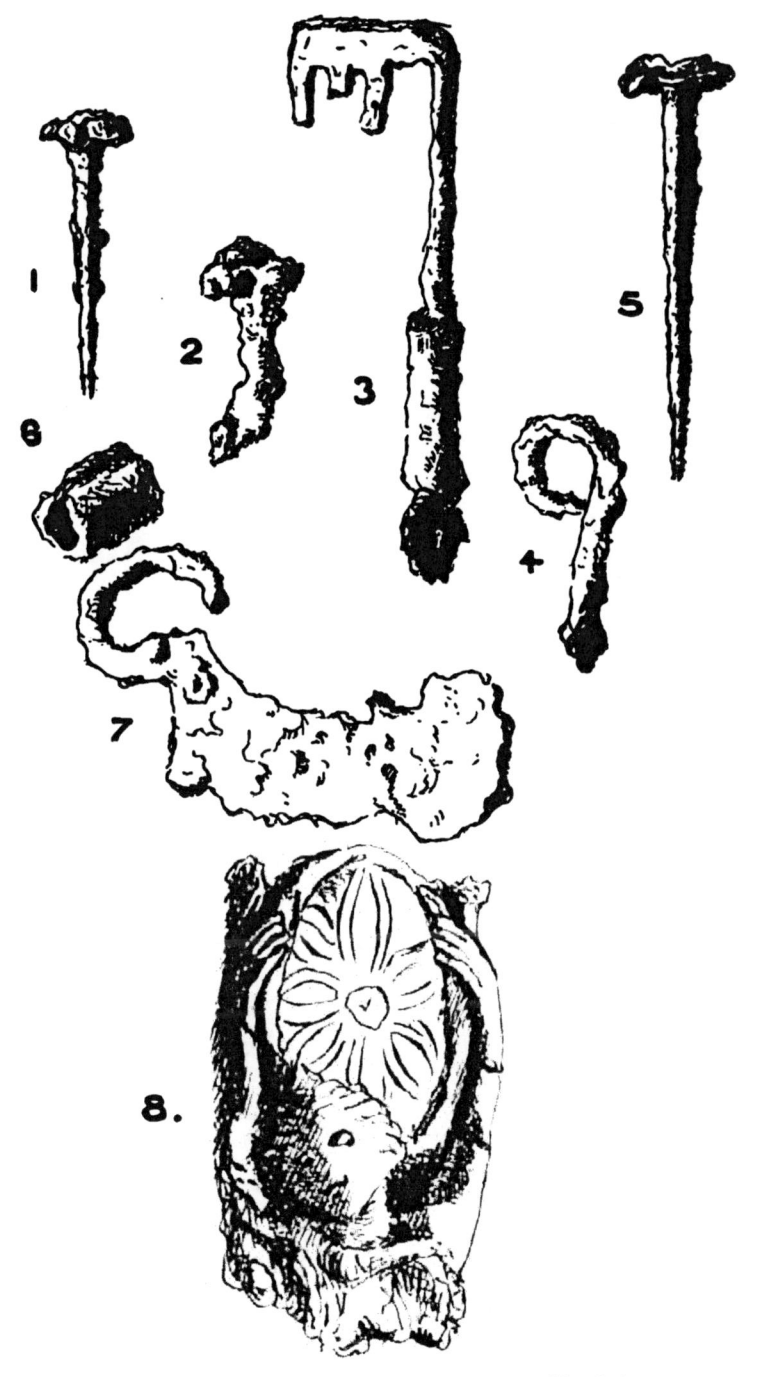

Sketched by Miss A. Airy.

1, 2 & 5.—ROMAN NAILS.   3.—ROMAN KEY.   4.—HOOK.
6.—FERRULE.   7.—HIPPO SANDAL.   8.—CARVING ON IVORY.

purple, yellow, black, and brown. One pattern is particularly rich in colouring, having narrow bands of blue, white, brown pencilled with a black margin, grey, red, and ochre; while another represents a floral design painted with a free brush.

Some specimens are interesting, as showing the process of repair, or second colouring, by the application of a fresh coat of plaster.

MISCELLANEOUS.—Masses of mortar and concrete, some evidently cast in round and triangular shapes, for corners of the building.

Quantities of loose tesseræ, generally plain, and about an inch square. Several were small, black and white, and beautifully polished, showing that in all probability fine mosaic floors once existed.

Clinker material.

A ring of pottery 2 inches in diameter.

A round disc of black pottery, with well worn hole in centre, evidently used for games.

Stone, hammer-shaped.

Tiles with impressions of fingers and the feet of various animals.

Oolite slabs, several worked.

Part of strainer.

Tiles with diamond pattern probably for cutting into tesseræ.

Part of cornice.

COINS.—Upwards of three hundred coins have been found, the dates ranging from 35 B.C. to 423 A.D. The majority are in an excellent state of preservation, while a few are hardly decipherable. They were found wherever excavations took place, but principally on the mound where the villa stood, and at all depths from one foot to fully four feet. Barbarous British imitations of Roman coins were found.

The following complete list of the various types has been kindly compiled by Mr. E. H. Tugwell, F.S.M.C., M.P.S., &c., to whom we are greatly indebted for deciphering and classifying them, and also for valuable assistance during the course of the excavations :—

LIST OF COINS

Found in Greenwich Park

during the excavations.

MARCUS ANTONIUS. Mark Antony, born about B.C. 83. Being defeated with Cleopatra, by Octavius Cæsar, at the battle of Actium, he fled to Egypt, where he slew himself in the same year, B.C. 31.

1. Obverse: A Prœtorian galley propelled by rowers, ANT. AVG . III . VIR . RP . C. (Antonius Augur Triumvir Reipublicæ Constituendae.)
    Reverse: The legionary eagle on a pike between two military standards.
    A denarius of the XIV. legion, struck at Alexandria, circ. B.C. 35.

CLAUDIUS I. Tiberius Claudius Drusus, born at Lyons, B.C. 10. He became emperor upon the death of Caligula, A.D. 41, and was poisoned by his wife, A.D. 54.

2. Obverse: Bust of the emperor to right. ... CAESAR. ...
    Reverse: A figure standing leaning on a spear. Inscription illegible. (2nd brass.)

LIST OF COINS.

NERO. Lucius Domitius Nero, born at Antium, A.D 37. Adopted by Claudius and created Caesar, A.D. 50. He became emperor, A.D. 54, and slew himself upon hearing that the soldiers had proclaimed Galba, A.D. 68.

3. Obverse: Bust of the emperor. Illegible. (1st brass.)
   Reverse: Figure in armour, marching.
   Inscription Illegible.
4. Obverse: Head of emperor.
   IMP. NERO. CAESAR.AVG.MAX.TR.P.P.I.
   See plate. (1st brass.)
   Reverse: A winged figure standing with hand resting on a buckler. In the field. S.C.

VESPASIAN. Flavus Vespasianus, born A.D. 9. Consul in Britain, A.D. 51. He was governor of Judea under Nero and became emperor, A.D. 69. Died A.D. 79.

5. Obverse: Head of emperor to right. ...VESP...AN. (1st brass.)
   Reverse: Figure of Aequitas standing. AEQVITAS. In the field. S.C.
6. Obverse: Head of emperor to right.
   CAESAR.VESPASIAN.AVG.COS IIII. IMP. (1st brass.)
   Reverse: Figure of Fortuna standing.
   FORTVNA . REBVCI. In the field. S.C.

TITUS. Titus Flavius Vespasianus, son of the Emperor Vespasian, born A.D. 41. He was associated with his father as Imperator, in A.D. 71, and succeeded him in the empire, A.D. 79. Poisoned by his brother, Domitian, A.D. 81.

7. Obverse: Laureated head of the emperor to right.
   T.CAES.IMP.AVG.F.PONT.R.P.COS. VI.CENSOR. (Very large brass.)
   Reverse: Figure of Virtue (?) standing.
   ROMA...VIRTVS. In the field. S.C.

78   GREENWICH PARK.

NERVA. Marcus Cocceius Nerva, born A.D. 32. He succeeded Domitian in the empire, A.D. 96, and died A.D. 98.

  8. Obverse: Laureated head of emperor to right
            IMP. NERVA. TRAIAN. AVG. GERM. P.M.
            See plate. (1st brass.)

     Reverse: A winged genius holding a label inscribed $_{Q.R.}^{S.P.}$
            TR. POT. COS III. P.P.
            In the field. S.C.

TRAJAN. Marcus Ulpius Trajanus, born at Italica, in Spain, A.D. 53. He was governor of Germania Inferior under Domitian and Nerva; created Caesar and Imperator by the latter in the year A.D. 97, and succeeded him as emperor, A.D. 98. Died in Cecilia, A.D. 117.

  9. Obverse: Bust of emperor. Inscription illegible.
            (1st brass.)
     Reverse: Illegible.

HADRIAN. Publius Aelius Hadrianus, born A.D. 76. Adopted by Trajan, and succeeded him, A.D. 117. Died at Baiae, A.D. 138.

 10. Obverse: Laureated head of emperor.
            IMP. CAESAR. TRAIANVS. HADRIANVS
            AVG. (1st brass.)
     Reverse: Figure of Britannia seated on a shield.
            ... TR. POT. COS III. A rare piece.

 11. Obverse: Laureated head of emperor.
            IMP. CAES. DIVI. TRA. PARTH. F. DIVI
            . NER. NEP. TRAIANVS. HADRIANVS.
            AVG.
     Reverse: Three standards.
            ... MAX. TER. POT. COS. VI.
            In the field. S.C. See plate. (1st brass.)

 12. Obverse: Laureated head of the emperor to right.
            ... HADRIANVS ... (1st brass.)
     Reverse: A figure standing. Illegible. In field. S.C.

LIST OF COINS.

13. Obverse: Laureated head of emperor. ...IVS...
    (2nd brass.)
    Reverse: Figure of (?) standing. Illegible.
    In the field. S.C.

14. Another (2nd brass), also illegible.

SABINA. Wife of Hadrian. Killed herself, A.D. 137.

14a. Obverse: Head of the Empress. (2nd brass.)
    Reverse: Figure standing holding the hasta pura.
    Illegible. In field. S.C.

ANTONINUS PIUS. Titus Aurelius Arrius Antoninus, born A.D. 86. Adopted by Hadrian, and succeeded him, A.D. 138. Died in Etruria, A.D. 161.

15. Obverse: Head of the emperor to right.
    Inscription illegible. (1st brass.)
    Reverse: Figure of Ceres.

16. Obverse: Laureated head to right.
    ANTONINVS . AVG . PIVS . P P . TR . P COS . III. (1st brass.)
    Reverse: Genius standing holding a branch and staff.
    GENIO . SENATVS. In field. S.C.

17. Obverse: Laureated head to right.
    ANTONINVS . AVG . PIVS . P . P . TR . P . COS . IIII. (1st brass.)
    Reverse: Nude figure wearing a helmet, holding a spear in the right hand and carrying a———(?) over his shoulder. S.C.

18. Obverse: Laureated head to right.
    ANTONINVS . AVG . PIVS . P . P. (1st brass.)
    Reverse: Figure standing holding two standards.
    ... POT . XIX . COS ...

19. Obverse: Laureated head to right.
    ANTONINVS . AVG . PIVS . P . P. (1st brass.)
    Reverse: Figure standing. ...PERA... Illegible.
    In the field. S.C.

FAUSTINA THE ELDER. Annia Galeria Faustina, wife of Antoninus Pius; married to him before he became emperor. Died A.D. 141.

20. Obverse: Head of empress [DIVA . FAV]STINA.
    (2nd brass.)
    Reverse: Female figure standing holding a globe and staff. AETERNITAS. In the field. S.C.

21. Obverse: Head of the empress.
    DIVA . AVGVSTA . FAVSTINA.
    See plate. (2nd brass.)
    Reverse: Female figure standing. PIETAS. In field. S.C.

MARCUS AURELIUS. Marcus Annius Verus Catilius Severus, adopted by Antoninus, and succeeded him in the empire, A.D. 161, taking the names of Marcus Aurelius Antoninus. He died at Vindobona (Vienna), A.D. 180.

22. Obverse: Laureated head of the emperor to right.
    IMP . M . ANTONINVS . AVG . TR . P . XXV.
    (1st brass.)
    Reverse: A laurel garland enclosing
    PRIMI . DECENNALES . COS . III . S . C.
    (Scarce.)

COMMODUS. Lucius Aelius Aurelius Commodus Antoninus, son of Marcus Aurelius, born A.D. 161. Created Caesar, A.D. 166; Imperator, A.D. 176; Augustus, A.D. 177; and succeeded to the empire, A.D. 180. He was poisoned by his concubine, Martia, and afterwards strangled by a wrestler, A.D. 192.

23. Obverse: Head of the emperor to right.
    . . . COMMODVS . ANTONINVS . AVG.
    See plate. (2nd brass.)
    Reverse: Female figure bearing a cornucopia. Illegible. In field. C.S.

PLAUTILLA. Fulvia Plautilla, wife of the emperor Caracalla, married A.D. 202, and exiled to the Lipari Islands in the following year, where she was put to death by his command in A.D. 212.

24. Obverse: Bust of the emperor to right.
    PLAVTILLA . AVGVSTA.
    A denarius (silver).
    Reverse: The empress holding a child on the left arm and grasping the hasta in the right hand.
    PIETAS . AVGG. (In fine condition.)

GORDIANUS III. Marcus Antonius Gordianus, son of Gordianus Africanus the Younger; became emperor upon the death of Balbinus and Pupienus, A.D. 238. Murdered at the instigation of Philip, the Praetorian prefect, A.D. 244.

25. Obverse: Radiated head of emperor.
    IMP . CAES . M . ANT . GORDIANVS . AVG.
    Reverse: The emperor standing holding a spear and sword. VIRTVS . AVG.
    A silver denarius (large size) in fine condition. Weight 78 grains.

GALLIENUS. Publius Licinius Gallienus, son of the Emperor Valerianus, associated in the empire with his father, with the titles of Caesar and Augustus, A.D. 253. After the capture of Valerianus by the Persians, he reigned alone until A.D. 268, when he was murdered by his soldiers near Milan.

26. Obverse: Radiated head of the emperor to right.
    [IMP . GALLIEN]VS . AVG. (3rd brass.)
    Reverse: A griffin walking.
    APOLLONI . CONS . AVG. See plate.

27. Obverse: Radiated head of the emperor to right.
    IMP . GALLIENVS . AVG. (3rd brass.)
    Reverse: Fortuna standing. FORTVNA . REDVX.

G

POSTUMUS. Marcus Cassianus Latinius Postumus, born in Gaul, of which province he was governor under Valerianus; he usurped the purple in A.D. 258, but was killed during a mutiny of his soldiers, A.D. 265.

28. Obverse: [IMP . C .] POSTVMVS . AVG.   A base silver denarius.

    Reverse: Figure of fortuna.   FORTVNA.

VICTORINUS. Marcus Piauvonius Victorinus. General under Postumus, and succeeded to his usurped purple, about A.D. 265. He was killed by his soldiers at Cologne, A.D. 267.

29. Obverse: Radiated head of the emperor to right.
    IMP . C . VICTORINVS . P . F . AVG.
    See plate.

    Reverse: The sun marching with right hand raised, and a whip (?) in the left.
    INVICTVS.   In field.   A star.

30. Obverse: Radiated head of the emperor.
    IMP . VICTORINVS . P . F . AVG.

    Reverse: Figure of fortuna.

31. Obverse: Radiated head of emperor to right.
    IMP . VICTORINVS . P . F . AVG.
    (3rd brass.)

    Reverse: Figure standing holding a torch (?) and the hasta pura.
    In the field.   Two stars.   Inscription illegible.

TETRICUS THE ELDER. Caius Pesuvius Tetricus. Usurper in Gaul. The legions elected him emperor upon the death of Victorinus. Tetricus maintained his sovereignty from A.D. 267, during the reigns of Gallienus, Claudius Gothicus, and part of that of Aurelian, when he voluntarily gave up the province and retired into private life, A.D. 272.

32. Obverse: Radiated head of the emperor to right.
   IMP . TETRICVS . AVG.
   Reverse: Victory standing holding a branch.
   COMES . AVG . N.   A scarce piece.

33. Obverse: Radiated head of emperor to right. Illegible.
   Reverse: Providence standing holding a cornucopia.
   PROVID . AVG.

34. Obverse: Radiated head of emperor to right.
   IMP . TETRICVS .   (3rd brass.)
   Reverse: A figure standing holding a necklace (?) and the hasta. Illegible.

35. Obverse: Radiated head to right.
   IMP . TETRICVS . P . F . AVG. (3rd brass.)
   Reverse: Peace standing. PAX.

36. Obverse: Radiated head to right.
   IMP . TETRICVS . P . F . AVG. (3rd brass.)
   Reverse: A female standing holding a flower and a cornucopia. HILARITAS . AVGG.

NOTE.—Several contemporary forgeries were found of this emperor that had evidently passed as current coin.

TETRICUS THE YOUNGER. Caius Pesuvius Pivesus Tetricus, son of Tetricus the Elder; created Caesar by his father in A.D. 266, and retired with him into private life, A.D. 272.

37. Obverse: Head of Tetricus.
   C . PIV . TETRICVS . C . AVG. (3rd brass.)
   Reverse: Pontifical vases.
   PIETAS . AVGG.   A scarce reverse.

38. Obverse: Radiated head to right.
   C . PIVESV . TETRICVS . C . AVG.
   (3rd brass.)
   Reverse: Female figure standing. Illegible.

39. Obverse: Radiated head to right.
C . PESV . TETRICVS . CAES.   (3rd brass.)

Reverse: Hope marching.   SPES . AVGG.   Scarce.

CLAUDIUS GOTHICUS.   Marcus Aurelius Claudius, born in Illyria, of obscure family, he was governor of that province under Gallienus, and upon the death of that emperor, was elected Augustus by the Legions and Senate, A.D. 268. He obtained his surname by a victory over the Goths, and died of the plague, A.D. 270.

40. Obverse: Radiated head of the emperor to right.
IMP . CLAVDIVS . AVG.   (3rd brass.)

Reverse: Figure of Venus standing.   VENVS.

41. Obverse: Radiated head of the emperor to right.
(3rd brass.)

Reverse: Illegible.

PROBUS.   Marcus Aurelius Probus, born in Pannonia, A.D. 232. The legions of the east proclaimed him emperor upon the death of Tacitus, A.D. 276. Probus was killed by his soldiers, A.D. 282, at his native town, Sirmium.

42. Obverse: Head of the emperor.
IMP . PROBVS . AVG.   (3rd brass.)

Reverse: Emperor on horseback with captives.
ADVENTVS . AVG.

43. Obverse: Radiated head of the emperor.
PROBVS . P . F . AVG.   (3rd brass.)

Reverse: Emperor on horseback, a captive on the ground. In the exergue P . ⊙ . Z.   (Struck at Rena.)

CARAUSIUS.   Marcus Aurelius Valerius Carausius, born in Gaul of obscure parents. He was appointed admiral of the Roman fleet stationed at Boulogne. Revolting against **Maximianus**, in A.D. 287, he sailed over to Britain, where he assumed the purple and title of Augustus. Unable to cope with him, the emperor acknowledged him as his colleague. He repulsed the Caledonian tribes, and with his fleet swept the seas, but was murdered by his own general, Allectus, A.D. 293.

44. Obverse: Radiated head of emperor to right.
    IMP . C . CARAVSIVS . P . P . AVG.
    (3rd brass.)

    Reverse: Figure of peace.   PAX.
    Struck in London. A rare coin.

HELENA. Flavia Julia Helena, the first wife of Constantius Chlorus and mother of Constantine the Great. She was divorced to make way for Theodora, and died about A.D. 328. The coins bearing her name were probably struck in her honour by Constantine the Great, circ. A.D. 330.

45. Obverse: Head of the empress to right.
    FL . IVL . HELENA . AVG.   (3rd brass.)

    Reverse: Woman holding a branch in the right hand and the hasta pura transversely in the left.
    PAX . PVBLICA.   In the exergue TR . P.

THEODORA. Flavia Maxima Theodora, married to Constantius Chlorus as his second wife, A.D. 292.

46. Obverse: Head of empress.
    FL . MAX . THEODORA . AVG.   (3rd brass.)

    Reverse: The empress nursing a child.
    PIETAS . ROMANA.   In the exergue TR . S.

MAXIMINUS DAZA. Galerius Valerius Maximinus, surnamed Daza, nephew of Maximinianus, was declared Caesar by Diocletian, and Augustus in

A.D. 305. He assumed the purple, A.D. 308, as Emperor of the East, but was defeated in battle by Licinius and fled to Tarsus, where he died, possibly by poison, A.D. 313.

47. Obverse: Head to right.
    IMP . MAXIMINVS . P . F . AVG.
    (3rd brass has been silvered.)

    Reverse: Genius standing holding the patera.
    GENIO . POP . ROM.

LICINIUS. Publius Flavius Claudius Galerius Licinianus Licinius, the son-in-law of Constantius Chlorus, was created Caesar and Augustus, A.D. 307, and ruled conjointly with Maximianus. In A.D. 313, he married Constantia, sister of Constantine the Great, the Emperor of the West. His cruel persecution of the Christians caused Constantine, who professed that religion, to declare war against him. Licinius was worsted and fled to Thessalonica, where he was strangled, A.D. 324.

48. Obverse: Bust of the emperor to right.
    IMP . LICINIVS . P . F . AVG.
    (Size of 3rd brass, but has been silvered.)

    Reverse: Genius standing wearing the modius on his head and holding a patera and the chlamys.
    GENIO . POP . ROM.
    In the field. T . F. In the exergue. P . TR.

CONSTANTINE THE GREAT. Flavius Galerius Valerius Constantinus, son of Constantius Chlorus and Helena; said to have been born in Britain, was proclaimed emperor at York, by the Legions, upon the death of his father at that place, A.D. 306. He professed the

LIST OF COINS.   87

Christian religion, A.D. 311. Being offended by the citizens of Rome, he removed the seat of government to Byzantium in A.D. 330, and re-named it Constantinopolis. He died in Bithynia, A.D. 337.

49-53. Obverse: Laureated head to right.
IMP . CONSTANTINVS . P . F . AVG.
(3rd bronze.)

Reverse: The sun standing holding a globe.
SOLI . INVICTO . COMITI.
In the field. TF. Others with nothing.
In the exergue. TR . P. Others with B . ⋈ . D.
or P . LG. or A . TR.

54. Obverse: Helmeted head to left.
CONSTANTINVS . F . AVG . C. (3rd brass.)

Reverse: The emperor standing between two standards.
PRINCIPI . INVENTVTVS.
In the field. A star. In the exergue. P . LN.
Scarce.

55. Obverse: Helmeted head to left.
CONSTANTINVS . FL . AVG. (3rd brass.)

Reverse: A globe surmounted by 3 stars, resting on an altar inscribed $\begin{smallmatrix}VOT\\IS\\XX\end{smallmatrix}$ ... NQ ... LITAS.
In the exergue. P . LON.

56. Obverse: Laureated head to right.
CONSTANTINVS . AVG .   (3rd brass.)

Reverse: A globe surmounted by 3 stars resting on an altar inscribed—
$\begin{smallmatrix}VOT\\IS\\XX\end{smallmatrix}$. BEATA . TRANQVILLITAS.
In the exergue. P . TR.

57. Obverse: Head of the emperor to right.
CONSTANTINVS . MAX . AVG. (3rd brass.)

GREENWICH PARK.

Reverse: A woman standing holding a branch in her right hand and the hasta pura transversely in her left. PAX . PVBLICA. See plate. Probably unique.

NOTE.—The reverse is the same as on the coins of his mother, Helena. See page 80.

58-9. Obverse: A head, wearing a Roman helmet, to left.
VRBS . ROMA. See plate. (3rd brass.)

Reverse: Romulus and Remus suckled by a wolf.
In the exergue. ISIS. or T . LC. (Lyons).

60-1. Obverse: A head, wearing a Roman helmet, to left.
CONSTANTINOPOLIS. (3rd brass.)

Reverse: Victory marching, holding a spear and a shield.
In the field. A wreath. In the exergue TR . P.
or TR . S. (Treves).

62-3. Obverse: Head of the emperor to right.
CONSTANTINVS . MAX . AVG.
(3rd brass.)

Reverse: Two soldiers holding spears, facing two standards. GLORIA . EXERCITVS.
In the exergue. P . CONS. (Constantinople),
or TR . S (Treves).

64. Obverse: Veiled head of the emperor.
DIV . CONSTANTINVS . P . T . AVGGI.
(3rd brass.)

Reverse: A soldier driving a quadriga. See plate.

65. Obverse: Helmeted head of emperor to right.
CONSTANTINVS . AVG. (3rd brass.)
Reverse: Two victories holding a wreath inscribed $\genfrac{}{}{0pt}{}{VOT}{S}$ supported on a cippus.
VICTOR . . . In the exergue. S . TR. (?)

66. Obverse: Head of the emperor.
CONSTANTIN (3rd brass.)
Reverse: A garland inscribed $\genfrac{}{}{0pt}{}{VOT}{XX}$.
CONSTANTIN . MAX . AVG.

LIST OF COINS. 89

67. Obverse: Head of the emperor.
CONSTANTINVS . AVG.   (3rd brass.)

Reverse: Victory placing a foot on a captive on the ground.   SARMATIA . DEVICTA.
In the exergue. P . LON. (Struck in London; scarce with these letters.)

68. Obverse: Head of the emperor.
CONSTANTINVS . MAX . AVG.
See plate.   (3rd brass.)

Reverse: Two soldiers grasping spears, facing a labarum surcharged with the monogram of Christ.

68A. Obverse: Veiled head of Constantine.
D . N . CONSTANTINVS . P . F . AVGG.

Reverse: The emperor standing wearing a toga.
VN . MR.
(3rd brass, the size of a quinarius. Rare.)

68B. Obverse: Head of the emperor.
CONSTANTINVS . AVG.

Reverse: Gate of the Prætorian Camp.
PROVIDENTIA . AVG.   (3rd brass.

68C. Obverse: Youthful head to left, with cornucopia.
POP . ROMANVS.

Reverse: A bridge supported on boats, with a tower at each end.
CONS . F.   (3rd brass. Rare.)

CRISPUS. Flavius Julius Crispus, son of Constantine the Great, created Caesar by his father, A.D. 317, and put to death by his orders upon a false accusation, A.D. 326.

69. Obverse: Head of Crispus.
IVL . CRISPVS . NOB . C.   (3rd brass.)

Reverse: A wreath enclosing $\genfrac{}{}{0pt}{}{VOT}{X}$.

70. Obverse: Laureated head to right.
    CRISPVS . CAESAR.   (3rd brass.)

    Reverse: Laurel garland enclosing IIOT
    ✥

    Inscription illegible.

70A. Obverse: Bust of Crispus holding a globe, surmounted by a staff tipped with a Victory?
    IVL . CRISPVS . NOB . CAES.

    Reverse: A globe surmounted by three stars, supported by an altar inscribed
    VOT
    IS
    XX
    BEATA . TRANQVILLITAS.
    In the exergue. P . TR.

CONSTANTINUS II. Flavius Claudius Julius Constantinus, son of Constantine the Great. He was created Caesar at the same time as Crispus, and upon the division of the empire by Constantine the Great, A.D. 335, received the provinces of Britain, Gaul, and Spain; at his father's death, the senate proclaimed him emperor. A quarrel with his brother Constans ended in a war; Constantine being defeated and killed near Aquileia, A.D. 340.

71. Obverse: Bust of Constantine as Caesar.
    CONSTANTINVS . IVN . N . C.   (3rd brass.)

    Reverse: Two soldiers facing a labarum.
    GLORIA . EXERCITVS.
    In the exergue TR . S.

72-3. Obverse: Bust of Constantine as emperor.
    CONSTANTINVS . IVN . AVG.   (3rd brass.)

    Reverse: Two soldiers, each holding a spear and standard with a wreath between them.
    GLORIA . EXERCITVS.
    In the exergue. P . CONST.
    On others P . LC. (Lyons).

LIST OF COINS. 91

74. Obverse: Bust of Constantine.
CONSTANTINVS . IVN . NOB. (3rd brass.)
Reverse: Two soldiers facing a labarum.
GLORIA . EXERCITVS.
In the exergue. P . L . S.

75. Obverse: Radiated head of Constantine to the left.
CONSTANTINVS . IVN . N . C.
Reverse: Votive altar inscribed VOT IS XX surmounted by a globe.
BEATA . TRANQVILLITAS.
In the field. PR. In the exergue. P . LON.
(Struck in London).

NOTE.—A coin the size of the 3rd brass, but has been silvered.

CONSTANS. Flavius Julius Constans, son of Constantine the Great. Upon the division of the empire by the latter, A.D. 337, he received the government of Italy, Illyria and Africa; and by the death of his brother, Constantine II., became sole Emperor of the West. Constans was murdered by the adherents of the usurper, Magnentius, A.D. 350.

76. Obverse: Head of the emperor.
CONSTANS . P . F . AVG. (3rd brass).
Reverse: A phœnix standing on a globe.
FEL . TEMP . REPARAT.
In the exergue. TR . S.

77. Obverse: Head of the emperor.
D . N . CONSTANS . P . F . AVG. (3rd brass.)
Reverse: A phœnix standing on a pyramid of globes.
FEL . TEMP . REPARAT.

78-84. Obverse: Head of the emperor.
CONSTANS . P . F . AVG. (3rd brass.)

92   GREENWICH PARK.

Reverse: Two victories standing facing and holding up wreaths.
VICTORIAE . DD . AVGG . Q . NN.
In the field. A palm branch. On others a ✳ or a heart, or Ḋ., or M.
In the exergue. TR . P. On others TR . S.

Note.—There are many varieties of this general design.

85. Obverse: Head of the emperor.
CONSTANS . P . F . AVG   (3rd brass.)

Reverse: Two soldiers facing a labarum.
GLORIA . EXERCITVS.
In the exergue. TR . S.

86. Obverse: Head of the emperor.
CONSTANS . P . F . AVG.   (3rd brass.)

Reverse: Figure holding a palm branch and the hasta pura transversely. Illegible.
In the exergue. L.

87. Obverse: Bust of the emperor to left, holding a globe in the right hand.
D . N . CONSTANS . P . F . AVG.
(2nd brass.)

Reverse: Soldier with a spear in his left hand, leading a child (?) from a hut under a cluster of wheat ears.
FEL . TEMP . REPAPATIO.
In the exergue. A I ☽.

88. Obverse: Bust of the emperor to right.
CONSTANS . P . F . AVG.   (3rd brass.)

Reverse: Two victories holding up garlands over a heart.
VICTORIAE . DD . NN . AVGVS.
In the exergue. OSTR^V. (Ostria).

CONSTANTIUS II. Flavius Julius Constantius, son of Constantine the Great, Created Caesar in A.D. 323, and on the death of his father, A.D. 337, received the provinces of the East as his share.

LIST OF COINS. 93

He became sole emperor upon the murder of Constans in A.D. 350, and died near Tarsus, A.D. 361.

89. Obverse: Bust of the emperor.
    D . N . CONSTANTIVS . P . F . AVG.
    (Small silver, weight 32 grains.)

    Reverse: Laurel garland enclosing
    ```
    VOTIS
     XXX
    MVLTIS
    XXXX
    ```
    In the exergue. S . CON.

90. Obverse: Bust of the emperor.
    D . N . FL . CONSTANTIVS. (3rd brass.)

    Reverse: Security standing with crossed legs leaning on a column, holding the hasta in the right hand.
    SECVRITAS . REIPVBLICAE.

91. Obverse: Bust of the emperor.
    FL . IVL . CONSTANTIVS . AVG.
    (3rd brass.)

    Reverse: Figure standing holding the hasta.
    AVGG . NN . . .

92-93. Obverse: Bust of the emperor.
    D . N . CONSTANTIVS . P . F . AVG.
    (2nd and 3rd brass.)

    Reverse: A soldier standing on a shield, spearing another on the ground.
    FELIX . TEMP . REPARATIO.
    In the exergue. P . LC.

NOTE.—A large number of contemporary forgeries of barbarous manufacture, of this coin were found.

94. Obverse: Bust of the emperor.
    D . N . CONSTANTIVS . P . F AVG.
    (3rd brass.)

    Reverse: A phœnix standing on a globe.
    FEL . TEMP . REPARATIO.
    In the exergue. TR . P.

95-97. Obverse: Bust of the emperor.
CONSTANTIVS . P . F . AVG. (3rd brass.)

Reverse: Two soldiers standing facing, a labarum between them.
GLORIA . EXERCITVS.
In the exergue. TR . S. And on others CONS. or P . LC. (Lyons).

98. Obverse: Bust of the emperor.
D . N . CONSTANTIVS . P . F . AVG.
See plate. (3rd brass.)

Reverse: The emperor standing on a galley, holding a globe surmounted by a phœnix, and a spear. A seated Victory rowing.
FEL . TEMP . REPARATIO.

99. Obverse: Bust of the emperor.
D . N . CONSTANTIVS. (3rd brass.)

Reverse: Two soldiers, each grasping a spear, facing a labarum.
GLORIA . EXERCITVS.
In the exergue. TR . S.

100. Obverse: Bust of the emperor.
CONSTANTIVS . P . F . AVG. (3rd brass.)

Reverse: Two victories holding wreaths.
VICTORIAE . DD . AVGG . Q . NN.
In the field a palm branch.
In the exergue. TR . S.

101. Obverse: Bust of the emperor.
FL . IVL . CONSTANTIVS . AVG.
(3rd brass.)

Reverse: Two soldiers holding spears, facing a standard.
GLORIA . EXERCITVS.
In exergue. TR . S.

MAGNENTIUS. Flavius Magnus Magnentius. A usurper, supposed to have been a British prisoner of war, who enlisted in the Roman legions and rose to the rank of general. He

LIST OF COINS.

seized the purple, A.D. 350, and caused the murder of Constans. Constantius II. offered him the provinces of Britain, Gaul, and Spain, but Magnentius refused the offer and, being defeated in the war that followed, fled to Lyons and stabbed himself, A.D. 355.

102. Obverse: Bare head of Magnentius to right.
D . N . MAGNENTIVS . P . F . AVG.
(2nd brass.) See plate.

Reverse: Two Victories supporting a garland charged
$\begin{matrix} \text{VOT} \\ \text{V} \\ \text{MVLT} \\ \text{X} \end{matrix}$ surmounted by the monogram of Christ

VICTORIAE . DD . AVG . ET . CAES.
In the exergue. ✱ . AM . B . ☋ . (Amiens).
In the field of the obverse. A.

103. The same design of obverse and reverse.
(3rd brass.) See plate.
In the exergue. R . P . L.—(Lyons).

DECENTIUS. Magnus Decentius, a brother of Magnentius. He was created Caesar by him, A.D. 351, and strangled himself upon hearing that Magnentius had been defeated and had died by his own hand, A.D. 353.

104. Obverse: Bust of Decentius to right.
D . N . DECENTIVS . NOB . CAES.
(3rd brass.)

Reverse: Two Victories supporting a garland. Illegible

104A. Obverse: D . N . DECENTIVS . NOB . CAES.

Reverse: Two Victories supporting a garland inscribed
$\begin{matrix} \text{VOT} \\ \text{V} \\ \text{MVLT} \\ \text{X} \end{matrix}$

VICTORIAE . DD . NN. . . .
In the field. S . P. In the exergue. RSLS.

VALENTINIANUS I. Flavius Valentinianus. He was general under Jovianus, upon whose death he became emperor, A.D. 364. After a reign of eleven years, Valentinian died in Pannonia, A.D. 375.

105. Obverse: Bust of the emperor to right.
   D . N . VALENTINIANVS . P . F . AVG.
   (3rd brass.)

   Reverse: The emperor holding the labarum in the left hand and dragging a captive by the hair.
   GLORIA . . . . .   In the exergue.   VC . S.

106. Obverse: Bust of the emperor.
   D . N . VALENTINIANVS . P . F . AVG.
   (3rd brass.)

   Reverse: The emperor standing, a labarum in his right hand and a branch in the left.
   Inscription illegible.   In the exergue.   CON.

107. Obverse: Bust of the emperor.
   D . N . VALENTINIANVS . P . F . AVG.
   (3rd brass.)

   Reverse: The emperor standing, a captive kneeling before him.
   REPARATIO . REIPVB.

108. Obverse: Bust of emperor.
   D . N . VALENTINIANVS . P . F . AVG.
   (3rd brass.)

   Reverse: The emperor with a labarum, hold a globe supporting a Victory.
   RESTITVTOR . REIP.
   In the exergue.   P . LVG.   (Lugdunum—Lyons)

109. Obverse: Bust of the emperor.
   D . N . VALENTINIANVS . P . F . AVG.
   (3rd brass.)

LIST OF COINS.

Reverse: Victory holding a wreath and branch.
SECURITAS . REIPVBLICAE.
In the field. O . P . L.
In the exergue. LVC . P.

VALENS. Flavius Valens, brother of Valentinian I. He was created Caesar and Augustus, A.D. 364, his brother giving him the Eastern Empire. Valens is supposed to have been burnt to death in A.D. 378.

110-11. Obverse: Bust of the emperor.
D . N . VALENS . P . F . AVG.   (3rd brass.)
Reverse: Victory marching.
SECVRITAS . REIPVBLICAE.
In the field. OF . N. Others with nothing.
In the exergue. P . CON.

112. Obverse: Bust of the emperor.
D . N . VALENS . P . F . AVG.
Reverse: Victory holding a wreath and palm branch.
SECVRITAS . REIPVBLICAE.
In the field. OF. and an inverted sickle. (?)
In the exergue. LVC . P. (Lyons 1st issue.)

THEODOSIUS THE GREAT succeeded Valens as Emperor of the East, A.D. 379. Died at Milan, A.D. 395.

113. Obverse: Bust to right.
D . N . THEODOSIVS . P F . AVG.
(3rd brass.)
Reverse: Victory Palmifera holding a wreath.
VICTORIA . AVGGG.
In the exergue. LVC . P.

GRATIANUS. Son of Valentinian I. He succeeded his father as Emperor of the West, A.D. 375. Gratianus was killed when fighting against Magnus Maximus, A.D 383.

H

114. Obverse: Head of the emperor to right.
D . N . GRATIANVS . P . F AVG.
(3rd brass.)

Reverse: Victory marching, holding a wreath and palm branch.
SECVRITAS . REIPVBLICAE.
In the field. OF III. In the exergue. CONS.

HONORIUS. Son of Theodosius I. He succeeded his father as Emperor of the West, A.D. 395, and died A.D. 423.

115. Obverse: Head of the emperor.
HONORIVS . AVGVSTVS. (3rd brass.)

Reverse: Illegible.

A CHRONOLOGICAL LIST.

A Chronological List of the 40 Emperors, etc., who are represented by coins found in the excavations:—

B.C.	35 (circ.)	Marcus Antonius.
A.D.	41-54	Claudius I.
,,	54-68	Nero.
,,	69-79	Vespasian.
,,	79-81	Titus.
,,	96-98	Nerva.
,,	98-117	Trajan.
,,	117-138	Hadrian.
,,	117-137	Sabina, wife of Hadrian.
,,	138-161	Antoninus Pius.
,,	141 *et seq.*	Faustina the Elder (wife of above).
,,	161-180	Marcus Aurelius.
,,	180-192	Commodus.
,,	202-203	Plautilla (wife of Caracalla).
,,	238-244	Gordianus III.
,,	253-268	Gallienus.
,,	258	Postumus, ⎫
,,	265-267	Victorinus, ⎬ Usurpers in
,,	267-272	Tetricus the Elder, ⎬ Gaul and Britain.
,,	267-272	Tetricus the Younger, ⎭
,,	268-270	Claudius Gothicus.
,,	276-282	Probus.
,,	287-293	Carausius (Usurper in Britain).
,,	292 (circ.)	Helena (wife of Constantius Chlorus).
,,	292 *et seq.*	Theodora (2nd wife of Constantius Chlorus).
,,	305-313	Maximinus Daza.
,,	307-324	Licinius.
,,	306-337	Constantine the Great.
,,	317-326	Crispus, ⎫
,,	337-340	Constantine II., ⎬ Sons of Constantine
,,	337-350	Constans, ⎬ the Great,
,,	337-361	Constantius II., ⎭ ruling concurrently.
,,	350-353	Magnentius (Usurper).
,,	351-353	Decentius (Caesar under Usurper).
,,	364-375	Valentinianus I.
,,	364-378	Valens.
,,	375-383	Gratianus.
,,	379-395	Theodosius I.
,,	395-423	Honorius.

The above dates point to a continuous and effective occupation of the site from A.D. 41, or shortly after, during the reign of Claudius I., who subjugated the south of Britain, to Honorious, A.D. 395-423, who finally recalled the legions from this country; the only great break being from Commodus to Gordianus, a period of forty-six years; but this has been partly bridged by a fine silver coin, found on almost the last day's digging, of Plautilla, wife of Caracalla, who reigned from A.D. 211-217. Two of the missing Emperors, viz.—Clodius Albinus and Severus, are known to have ruled personally in Britain—the latter died at York—so it is quite probable that their coins may yet be found when excavating is resumed.

The earliest coin yet unearthed is a denarius of Mark Antony, struck at Alexandria, circ. B.C. 35, for paying the soldiers of the 14th (Germina) legion, and as we know from history that this legion served in Britain in some of the earlier expeditions, it may possibly have been dropped by them when camping upon the spot that in after years became a permanent military (?) settlement, for the remains of two entrenched camps of Roman origin are still visible in immediate proximity.

The coin, although worn, is in far too good a state of preservation to have been in circulation for a period of 70 or 80 years, so that the balance of evidence points to the probability, as well as plausibility, of the above theory.

MISCELLANEOUS NOTES.

At what date the Park was thrown open to the public, has not been ascertained, but, in all probability, considerable freedom has been offered from the time of King George IV. About 1700, a pass to the Park was issued to persons living in the district, which allowed the holders to enjoy the quiet of the grounds, though as late as forty years ago the Park gates were locked at a uniform time each evening. The pass was of copper, the annexed illustration showing the actual size with the reverse and obverse sides.

REFERENCES TO GREENWICH PARK.

These are few; the most trustworthy to which I have had access being MSS. in the Record Office, Patent Rolls (33, Henry VI.), MSS. State Papers, Domestic MSS., Issues of the Exchequer, and files of papers connected with H.M.O. Works, in whose management the Park is vested. Many of the interesting notes contained in Drake's "Hundred of Blackheath," the "History of Lee," and "The

Beauties of England and Wales," have been obtained from the first four sources.

"Richardson's History of Greenwich," and a copy of the same, with MS. notes interleaved by the late Mr. Charles Kadwell, in the possession of Mr. J. Cabban, contain many valuable references to the Park.

The earliest sketches of the Park are, probably, Wyngaerdes (1558); copies of which may be seen in the Museum attached to the Royal Naval College. In the Royal Observatory there is a plan of the Park about the time of the planting of Blackheath avenue, and a Survey of the Park and Demesne-land, in 1695, by the Surveyor-General, both of particular interest as showing the Park at those early dates. There are several others of more recent times, particularly that published by the "London Magazine," about 1750. Of Greenwich Castle and tower, the best engravings are those contained in this book.

The Roman and other Remains

which have been found in the Park may be viewed on application to the Superintendent.

Games in Park.

The officers of the Royal Naval College, and boys of the Royal Hospital School, are alone allowed to play football in the Park. Hockey and cricket are not permitted. Two tennis courts are provided, on which about thirteen clubs can play each season. Permits for using these courts are necessary, and a secretary is appointed by the Superintendent, who makes arrangements as to days and hours of playing.